PLACES AND CASES
The World

Robert Prosser

Series Editor
Peter Webber

Stanley Thornes (Publishers) Ltd

Text © Robert Prosser 1998

Original illustrations © Stanley Thornes (Publishers) Ltd 1998

Designed by Peter Tucker, Holbrook Design (Oxford) Ltd

Illustrated by Hardlines, Tim Smith and TTP International

Picture research by Penni Bickle

Edited by Phebe Kynaston

Cover photo: Science Photo Library

First published in 1998 by:
Stanley Thornes (Publishers) Ltd
Ellenborough House
Wellington Street
CHELTENHAM GL50 1YW
England

98 99 00 01 02 / 10 9 8 7 6 5 4 3 2 1

A catalogue record for this book is available from the British Library.

ISBN 0-7487-2914-3

Printed and bound in Italy by STIGE, Turin

Acknowledgements

With thanks to the following for permission to reproduce photographs and other copyright material in this book:

Ecoscene p.85, Figure 11.17 ● Environmental Images: *Kam y Sung* p.85, Figure 11.15 ● Frank Lane Picture Agency: *Roger Tidman* p.75 ● Genesis p.77 ● Robert Gwynne p.62 ● Robert Harding: *David Lomax* p.78, *Fraser Hall* p.73 ● Impact Photos: *Mark Henley* p.51, Figure 7.3, *Colin Jones* p.32, Figure 4.7, *Tadashi Kajiyama* p.11, *Alan Keohane* p.39, *Alain Le Garsmeur* p.18, *Norman Lomax* p.30 ● Kyodo, Japan p.15 ● Life Science Images p.87 ● Rex Features p.9 ● Chris Ridgers p.55 ● Science Photo Library: *Distribution Spot Image* p.5 ● Still Pictures: *Lars Bahl* p.51, Figure 7.6 (right), *Helour Netocny* p.57, Figure 8.2, *Mike Schroder* p.80 ● Topham Picturepoint p.44 ● Travel Ink: *Derek Allan* p.82 ● Trip Photographic: *R Belbin* p.90, *S Grant* p.86, Figure 12.1, *Eric Smith* p.92, *J Sweeney* p.83, *A Tovy* p.81, *Ben Turner* p.22, *J Wakelin* p.57, Figure 8.3 ● Chas Wilder p.51, Figure 7.6 (left).

The following photographs were supplied by the author: pp.23; 26; 27; 28, Figure 3.11; 32, Figure 4.6; 42; 43; 50; 69; 72; 86, Figure 12.2.

Alaska Department of Fish and Game: p.35, Figure 14.4B ● American Geographical Society, for adapted material from *Geographical Review*, October 1995 by B J Godfrey: p.79, Figure 11.4; p.80, Figure 11.5 ● Gemini News Service: p.58, Figure 8.5 ● Government of the Gambia: p.76, Figure 10.8 ● Government of Mauritius: p.74, Figure 10.5 ● The Guardian: p.9, Figure 1.1 (24.1.95); p.10, Figure 1.4 (17.4.97); p.50, Figure 7.2 (left) (13.9.96); p.56, Figure 7.15 (right) (28.9.96) ● Hodder & Stoughton Educational, for extracts from *Managing Wilderness Regions*: p.43, Figure 5.9; p.45, Figure 5.14; p.88, Figures 12.4 and 12.5; p.89, Figure 12.6; p.91, Figure 12.9 ● The Independent: p.91, Figure 12.8 (5.12.97) ● International Federation of Red Cross and Red Crescent Societies: p.16, Figure 2.2 ● Reprinted with permission of the Miami Herald: p.21, Figure 2.11 (30.8.92) ● © National Geographic Society: *William H. Bond* p.12, *Cartographic Division* p.13 ● New Zealand Journal of Geography: pp.11–12, Figure 1.6 (April 1995) ● The Observer: p.30, Figure 4.2 (12.12.93); p.68, Figure 9.7 (15.6.97) ● State Statistical Bureau, China: p.70, Figure 9.14; p.71, Figure 9.15 ● Time: p.15, Figure 1.10 (22.1.96) ● © Times Newspapers Limited: p.45, Figure 5.13 (25.5.97); p.50, Figure 7.2 (right) (18.8.96) ● US Fish and Wildlife Service: p.23, Figure 3.2.

Every effort has been made to contact copyright holders. The publishers apologise to anyone whose rights have been inadvertently overlooked, and will be happy to rectify any errors or omissions.

Contents

Introduction

To the student

This book about the World is one in a series of three textbooks for GCSE Geography. One book covers the United Kingdom, while a second looks at European issues.

You will find that much of the book consists of case studies. There is some background information about a topic before many of the case studies are introduced. For example, the case study on pages 17–20 examines the monsoon climate of the Indian subcontinent. Before the case study, the materials get you to think about the climate and weather. However, if you are to make the best use of the case study, you need to know already about the main elements that make up weather. This is why there is a 'Do you know?' box in each unit. It is assumed that you use a 'core' geography textbook and will have had some class time to make sure you know the definitions and the answers to any questions in the 'Do you know?' box before you study the topics in this book. This case study approach allows you to deepen and broaden your knowledge and understanding.

The case studies have been chosen to cover the main topics you need for your GCSE syllabuses. So, you will find case studies on earthquakes, ecosystems, weather and climate, population, settlement, development and environmental issues. Most GCSE examinations either include case studies for you to analyse, or ask you to use a case study you have studied. This book, therefore, gives you practice and examples. You will find that the activities throughout the book will help you develop the different skills you need in examinations. These include using photographs, tables, graphs, maps, diagrams, charts, as well as reading sections of text and completing decision making exercises. This book gives you plenty of practice!

The symbol ➡ suggests that you write at greater length and in more detail. Your answer should be at least a paragraph in length.

The words which appear in bold throughout this book are key terms which are defined in the Glossary on pages 95 and 96.

Geography is all about how the world works – the natural world and the human world – and is about more than examinations. So, we hope this book will help you to take an interest in and begin to understand the world around you.

Enjoy your Geography!

Infrared satellite image of the Mekong Delta, southern Vietnam

Location of case studies

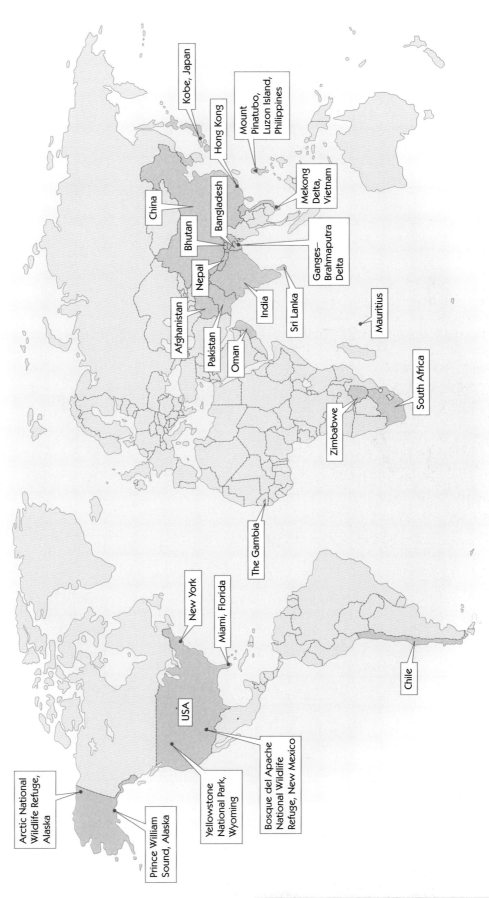

World natural regions

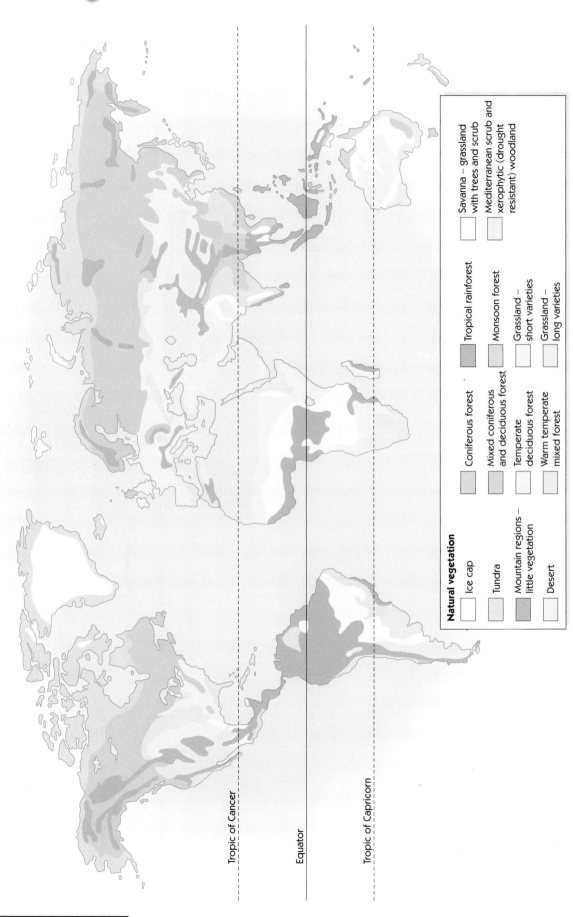

Natural vegetation

- Ice cap
- Tundra
- Mountain regions – little vegetation
- Desert
- Coniferous forest
- Mixed coniferous and deciduous forest
- Temperate deciduous forest
- Warm temperate mixed forest
- Tropical rainforest
- Monsoon forest
- Grassland – short varieties
- Grassland – long varieties
- Savanna – grassland with trees and scrub
- Mediterranean scrub and xerophytic (drought resistant) woodland

Tropic of Cancer

Equator

Tropic of Capricorn

World population

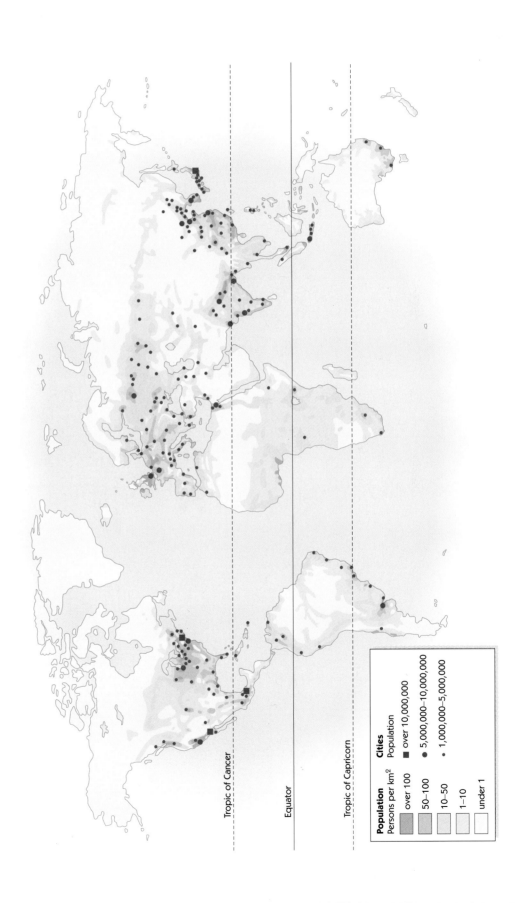

Population
Persons per km²

over 100
50–100
10–50
1–10
under 1

Cities
Population

■ over 10,000,000
● 5,000,000–10,000,000
• 1,000,000–5,000,000

Tropic of Cancer

Equator

Tropic of Capricorn

World economics and wealth

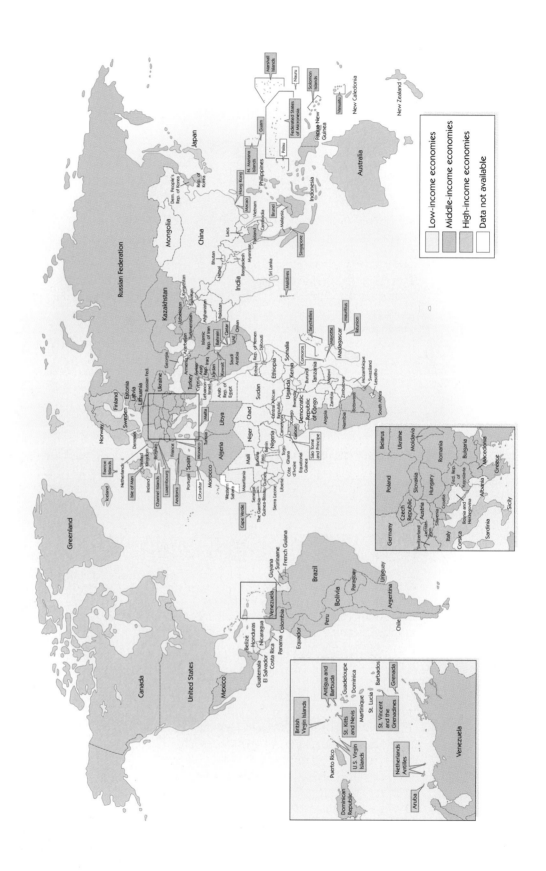

Low-income economies

Middle-income economies

High-income economies

Data not available

The unquiet crust

Main activity

Information interpretation.

Do you know?

❓ The earth's crust is built of a set of huge tectonic plates.
❓ These plates move slowly over the underlying mantle.
❓ Some pairs of plates move towards each other (subduction and collision margins), some pull apart (constructive margins), and some grind past each other (conservative margins).
❓ These movements at plate margins help to explain volcanic eruptions and earthquakes.
❓ Eruptions and earthquakes have three phases: before the main event; the event itself; after the event. The whole process may last many years.

Key ideas

● Volcanic eruptions and earthquakes are often violent, short-lived events. However, they may have both short- and long-term impacts upon human lives and activities.
● Prediction of eruptions and earthquakes is still uncertain.
● Eruption and earthquake hazards are concentrated along crustal plate margins.

Understanding earthquakes and eruptions

Can you remember the last time television news showed a volcanic eruption or the results of an earthquake? If you cannot remember, it may be because they occur so often that you hardly notice, or because they happen so far away that they seem remote.

Yet volcanic eruptions and earthquakes are part of the everyday life of planet earth. A research centre in Edinburgh records around 30,000 earth tremors a year from around the world. They are usually sudden and dangerous events which contain far more energy and force than nuclear explosions. They are serious hazards for many millions of people (Figure 1.1). Earthquakes have killed 1.4 million people during the twentieth century.

Date	Location	Richter scale magnitude	Fatalities
4.2.1996	Yunan, China	7.0	255
17.1.1995	Kobe, Japan	7.2	4400
15.2.1994	Indonesia	6.5	37
17.1.1994	Los Angeles, USA	6.6	57
30.9.1993	India	6.4	22,000
12.7.1993	Japan	7.8	26
12.12.1992	Indonesia	6.8	1912
28.6.1992	Monterey, California, USA	7.4	1
25.4.1992	California, USA	6.9	no deaths
13.3.1992	Turkey	6.8	1000
1.2.1991	Pakistan/ Afghanistan border	6.8	1200
16.7.1990	Philippines	7.7	1621
21.6.1990	Iran	7.3–7.7	50,000

Figure 1.1: Major earthquakes, 1990–96

So, in this unit we shall use examples to begin to answer several key questions about eruptions and earthquakes:
● What causes them?
● Why do they occur where they do?
● What effects do they have?
● Can we predict when they will occur?
● What can we do about them?

CASE STUDY: Living with volcanoes: Mount Pinatubo, Philippines

If you mark on a world map where volcanic eruptions and earthquakes occur over a number of years, a clear pattern emerges. Your map will show a set of lines and clusters running through continents and oceans. These indicate the zones where the great tectonic plates, which move slowly across the earth's crust, meet and pull apart. These are **plate margins**. The eruptions and earthquakes are brief, violent events. However, they may have long-term impacts upon people's lives. And they may occur again!

In the examples given in this case study, notice in particular:
● the enormous energy involved;
● the impacts on people, buildings and the environment;
● the short-term and longer-term impacts;
● the positive as well as the negative effects.

Figure 1.2: Mount Pinatubo: The event

After lying dormant for 600 years Mount Pinatubo, on Luzon island in the Philippines, exploded on 12–16 June 1991 in one of the largest eruptions of the century (Figure 1.2). This is a densely populated region, and over 200,000 people were evacuated and at least 1000 died. Only one-third of these died during the eruption itself. Many died later from diseases which spread through the evacuation camps. The rest have been killed by recurring mudflows, known as **lahars**.

The lahar legacy

The steep flanks of Mount Pinatubo have been blanketed by two types of deposit (Figure 1.3). First, there is the blanket of fine ash which fell from the sky to give layers up to 50 centimetres thick.

Second, there is the heavier ash and debris which poured as **pyroclastic** flows down the valleys radiating from the mountain. These deposits are up to 200 metres thick. Together these two types of deposit form an easily erodible blanket of loose material. When the monsoon rains arrive, disastrous lahars sweep down the valleys. These are likely to continue for many years, and explain why the death-toll is still rising.

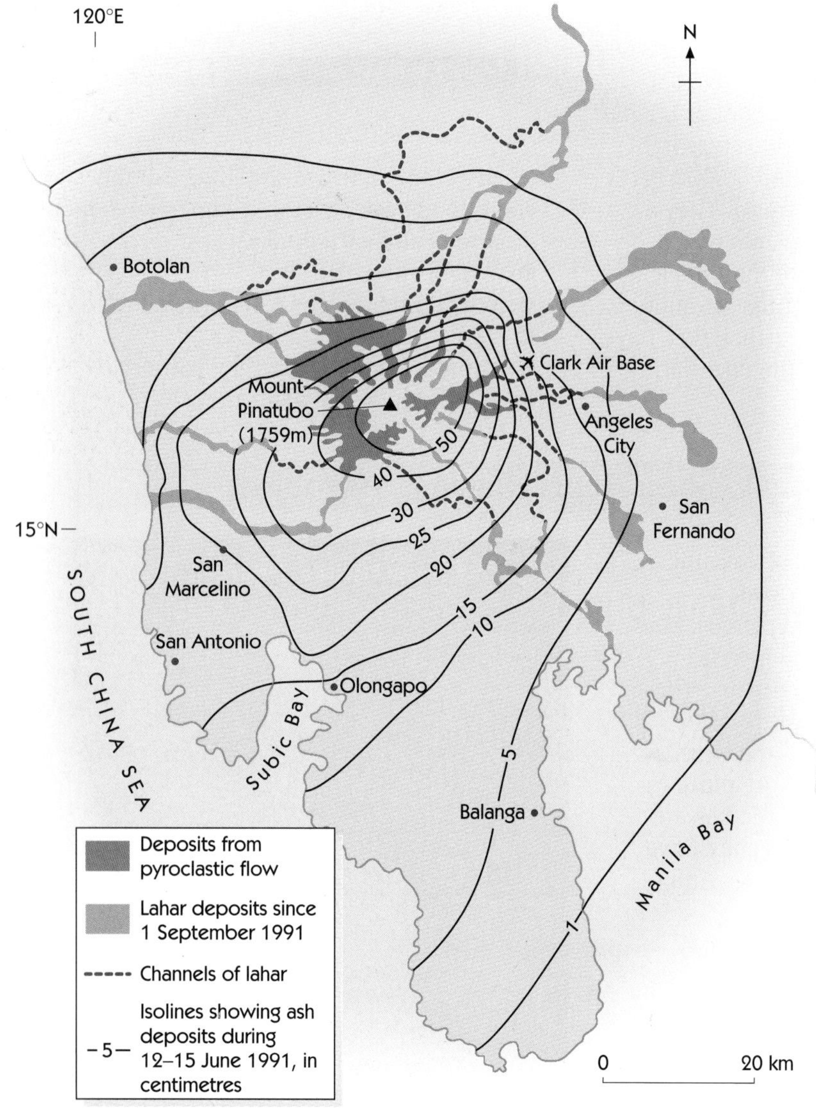

Figure 1.3: The impact of the eruption of Mount Pinatubo

RIVER OF SLUDGE CHOKES LIFE UNDER THE VOLCANO

After 600 years of dormancy, Mount Pinatubo exploded in June 1991 in one of the most destructive volcanic eruptions of the century. Its vast outpouring of concrete-like sludge has turned hundreds of square miles of surrounding farmland into a grey desert.

Scientists say these yearly inundations could continue for a decade, wiping out more towns and cities. Hundreds of thousands of people live in peril for miles around.

The old Spanish-era city of Bacolor, 25 miles [40 kilometres] from the mountain, survived until September 1995, when it too disappeared under more than 20ft [six metres] of hardened sludge, known as lahar to seismologists. A few roofs of the taller buildings remain, as if lying on the ground, some with signs for schools or banks or municipal offices. On the spots where their homes were buried they have built small shanties on stilts made of volcanic concrete, in case of future flows of sludge.

It is as if the surface of the earth around Mount Pinatubo has turned itself inside out. This new landscape, as deep as 30 or even 90 feet [nine or even 27 metres], is made up of volcanic ejecta, sand and feather-light pebbles and porous boulders from deep inside the mountain.

Vast amounts of the dry material still cover the mountain's slopes, its temperature as high as 495 degrees Fahrenheit [257 degrees centigrade]. When the monsoon comes each autumn, the material mixes with the water and begins to flow like concrete pouring from a delivery truck.

Lahar is a part of life in the refugee settlement of Dapdap, 60 miles [95 kilometres] from the Philippines capital Manila, where 10,000 people who fled the nearby town of Bamban live in drab hollow-block houses made from the same material that buried their homes.

Said Kelvin Rodolfo, a vulcanologist at the University of Chicago, 'No lahar flows of this magnitude and duration have ever been recorded.'

Figure 1.4: The impact of lahars

▼ Questions

1 For how long had Mount Pinatubo been dormant?

2 List the main impacts of the eruption upon:
   a people's lives (Figure 1.4);
   b the environment.

3 What is a 'lahar', what causes it, and where is a lahar most likely to occur?

The event

Mike Yalden's story (Figure 1.6) tells what happened in the city of Kobe at 5.46 a.m. on 17 January 1995. He was caught in what the Japanese have named the Great Hanshin Earthquake. The main tremors lasted less than one minute, but at least 5500 people died, 190,000 buildings were destroyed or damaged, and 300,000 people had to move to temporary shelters and camps (Figure 1.5).

As one magazine described:

'It toppled bridges, twisted highways, snapped ten-ton trucks like toothpicks and severed the trunk line of Japan's famous bullet train... It shut off water, gas and electricity to nearly 1 million households and scrambled the underground pipes so completely that thousands of people were still without gas three months later.'

Yet remember – earthquakes can bring even greater disaster. More than 143,000 people died in the 1923 Great Kanto Earthquake in the Tokyo area, while in Tangshan, China, at least 250,000 were killed in 1976.

Most deaths were caused by buildings collapsing and by fires which followed the main earthquake. Many families were cooking breakfast on paraffin stoves which were thrown over by the tremors.

Figure 1.5: Damage caused by the Kobe earthquake

Figure 1.6: Mike Yalden is an Australian businessman who experienced the Kobe earthquake. Here is his story.

5.46 a.m.

It is impossible for me to ever forget the very rude wake up call in my Kobe hotel at precisely 5.46 a.m. on Tuesday 17th January 1995... The most awful sounds of steel being stressed, coupled with the banging of building panels and the crash of moveable objects, all combined to make me painfully aware that I was in the middle of a nightmare. The endless violent shaking that accompanied the noise indicated that the nightmare was in fact an earthquake, 7.2 on the Richter scale and the worst in Japan since the early twenties.

Trying to stand was impossible in the first moments and any attempt resulted in an opposing force sending me crashing into some pieces of furniture or a wall. I could see the rolling surfaces of the room heaving and at times leaving cracks large enough to put your hand into only to find seconds later that they had closed again.

6.30 a.m.

The hotel staff were mustering everyone in the lobby. Continual aftershocks and raw fear prevented us from venturing outside and, since flying glass can be a major cause of casualties, we huddled in the lobby.

From 7.00 a.m.

We were still experiencing some quite severe aftershocks. It was amazing how you could hear them approach, a low rumble that came toward you at incredible speed, coinciding at the moment of arrival with more violent shaking. Somebody marked each time that one was felt and at the end of the day had given up counting at 600!

continued on page 12

The next day

The city centre: Many multi-storey buildings were leaning at crazy angles, in others the floors had collapsed on each other... The more damaged structures appeared to have been built in the sixties and seventies. More modern buildings seemed to have survived.

The suburbs: Mass destruction of homes, mostly old wooden houses, but also with a fair proportion of apartment blocks... Fire had taken its awful toll on those trapped in the wreckage of family homes.

The people: Survivors had set up camp in the nearest car park with what meagre belongings they were able to retrieve. Camp consisted of a blanket on the ground, huddled around a fire made from the shattered ruins. Piped water was generally non-existent but I noticed several hand operated pumps bringing water from old wells. Some shopkeepers were setting up stalls on pavements, selling foodstuffs... It was interesting and heartening to notice the complete lack of looting.

What caused the earthquake?

The Japanese learn to live with earthquakes. All schools have regular earthquake escape drills, road signs show escape routes, and the country spends £70 million a year trying to predict earthquakes. Figure 1.7 explains this concern. The four main islands of Japan – Hokkaido, Honshu, Shikoku, Kyushu – sit where four crustal plates meet.

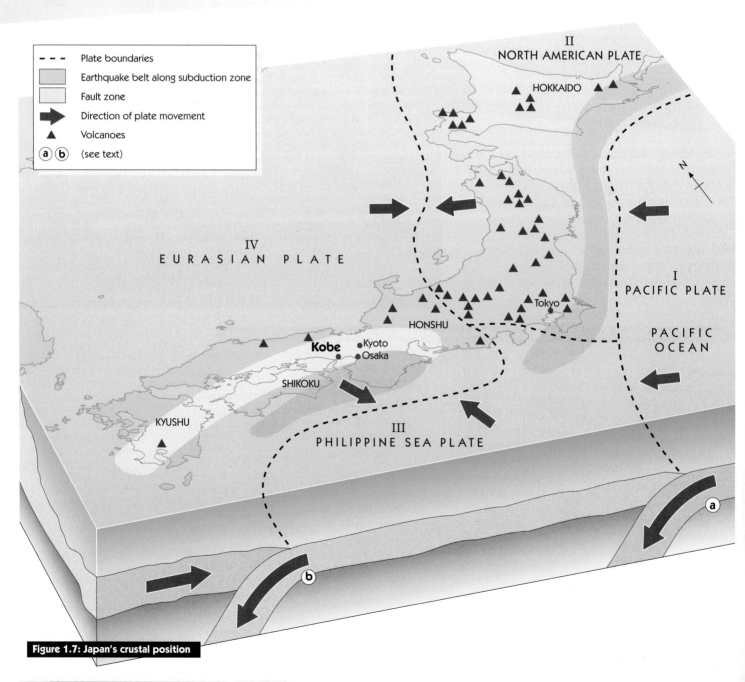

Figure 1.7: Japan's crustal position

Study Figure 1.7 carefully.

● The massive Pacific Plate is pushing west at a rate of about seven centimetres a year. It is forced under the North American and Philippine Sea Plates. This creates a subduction zone where one plate moves under another (**a** on the map), and explains the frequent earthquakes which occur to the east of Japan and the volcanoes in Hokkaido and Honshu.

● The smaller Philippine Sea Plate is driving north west beneath the eastward moving Eurasian Plate. This creates another subduction zone (**b** on the map).

● As a result, the crust has split in a series of faults running across Kyushu, Shikoku and into southern Honshu at Kobe and Osaka. This **fault zone** is made up of a number of faults where the crust is adjusting to the stresses caused by the plate movements.

It was a sudden movement along the Nojima Fault, in this fault zone, that caused the earthquake of 17 January 1995.

Like the other faults along this zone, the Nojima Fault had been 'quiet' for at least 50 years. By 'quiet', **seismologists** mean that few tremors had been recorded. This in fact is a danger signal along active plate margins, for it means that sections of a fault have locked against each other. The longer they remain locked, the more the tension builds up. In contrast, when plates judder regularly past each other, frequent minor tremors are recorded. So silence may be a warning!

The locked section of the Nojima Fault which snapped was 15 kilometres below the surface. This is its **hypocentre**. The **epicentre**, the surface point directly above the hypocentre, is in the middle of the Akashi Strait. The cross-section of Figure 1.8 tells us several important things about an earthquake. The fracture around the hypocentre triggers movement along other sections of the fault. For example, in the great 1906 San Francisco earthquake, movement occurred along a 60-kilometre section of the San Andreas Fault.

Most hypocentres occur well below the surface, although the tearing of the crust can be seen at the surface.

An earthquake is seldom a single, short-lived set of tremors, but may continue for days as a series of **aftershocks**. These are less severe tremors caused as sections of the two crustal plates continue to adjust. In Kobe, Mike Yalden was feeling the aftershocks which occurred along 50 kilometres of the fault zone.

Figure 1.8: Locating the Kobe earthquake

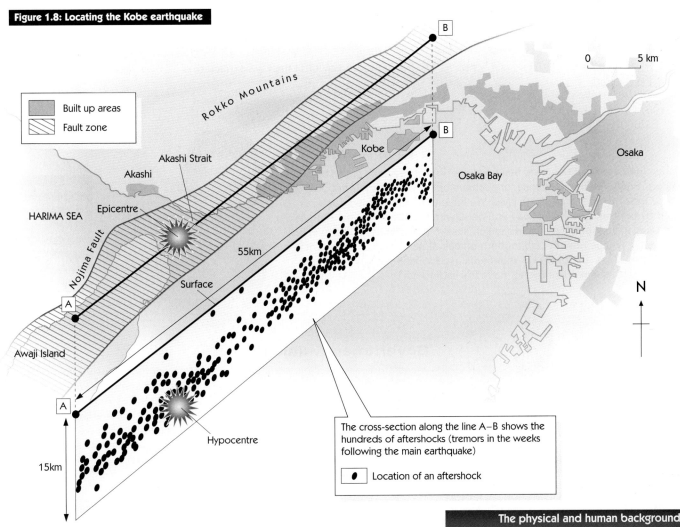

The cross-section along the line A–B shows the hundreds of aftershocks (tremors in the weeks following the main earthquake)

● Location of an aftershock

Figure 1.9

Why were so many people killed?

City planner

Japan is short of space. In cities like Kobe, people live crowded together at high densities. In older districts like Nagata, most houses were built of wood, often with heavy tile roofs. As the houses shook, the wooden frames were not strong enough and the roofs collapsed. This killed many people.

Fire officer

In most cases, the paraffin stoves started the fires. Then gas leaking from broken mains acted as fuel. The wooden buildings burned quickly and fiercely. Our biggest problem was lack of water. Because the pipes had broken, we had no supply for our hoses. Also, the roads were blocked or damaged and it was difficult to get our equipment there.

Why were there such disastrous fires?

Why did the earthquake take you by surprise?

Scientist

Two reasons really. First, the Nojima Fault had not caused trouble before. Second, our instruments often pick up warning signs such as minor tremors well before the main 'quake. This time there was very little warning, and it was a lot more powerful than we expected!

Civil engineer

Many older steel and concrete buildings are rigid. They can't stand being shaken strongly. So they collapse, or sections of the walls and floors break away. Today the city has tough laws. We have to build flexible structures with strong frames. These sway and bend with the shock waves. Bigger buildings have foundation blocks which absorb much of the shock wave energy. Notice how the tall modern offices of Kobe's business district didn't collapse. Buildings on sediments used to infill the bay collapsed because the shaking made the sediments lose their strength.

Why did so many taller buildings collapse or become badly damaged?

Can we prevent it happening again?

Government minister

Japan studies what is happening in the earth's crust more closely than any other country. But we are discovering new faults, and some we know still surprise us. Remember – the Northridge Earthquake in Los Angeles in 1994 occurred along a fault the Californian scientists did not know about! So, my answer is that we can't yet predict earthquakes accurately. But we can build earthquake-resistant buildings, and improve ways to prepare for and respond to earthquakes. Fewer people should be killed and the damage costs will be less.

Progress report – one year on

On the first anniversary of the earthquake, Kobe's mayor said: 'It will take five more years to finish rebuilding.' But although many thousands still lived in temporary homes, great progress had already been made (Figure 1.11).

Railroads: All 91.7 km of damaged track for the Shinkansen (bullet train) were restored by April 1995. All local train services resumed by June.

Buildings: Of the 62 major commercial buildings in central Kobe that were demolished, only 19 are scheduled for reconstruction so far. Another 122,500 structures were destroyed, but only 20,500 new applications to build or rebuild have been filed with authorities.

Business: Two-thirds of central Kobe's 11,650 shopkeepers have reopened their shops

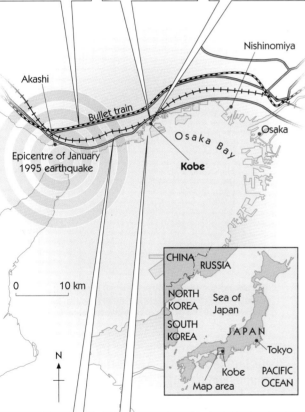

Highways: 27.7 km of the Hanshin Expressway, a major coastal artery, were damaged. Repairs will be completed in October, more than a year earlier than expected.

Shipping: At Kobe port, 30% of 230 damaged container berths have been repaired and traffic has been restored to 70% of its 1994 levels. The port is expected to be back to normal by 1997.

People: The death toll from the quake was 6,279 (4,512 in Kobe). More than 96,000 residents have moved elsewhere, lowering the city's population to 1.4 million.

Figure 1.10: Kobe: one year after

Figure 1.11: A The elevated Hanshin Expressway toppled over
B The rebuilt section one year later

▼ Questions

1 What do the terms 'epicentre', 'hypocentre' and 'subduction' mean? (Look carefully at Figures 1.7 and 1.8, and the text on page 13.)
2 Study Figure 1.1 on page 9. What rank does the Kobe earthquake have among recent major earthquakes?
3 How long did the main tremors from the Kobe earthquake last?
4 From the account of the event and Mike Yalden's story (Figure 1.6):
   a Make two lists:
      ● The physical damage to the city.
      ● The effects on the lives of people in Kobe.
   b Describe where most of the deaths occurred and explain why some areas suffered more than others.
   c What evidence is given of the enormous power of an earthquake?
5 What are aftershocks and why are they an important part of an earthquake event (Figures 1.6 and 1.8)?
6 What caused the earthquake and why did it surprise the scientists?
7 What can the Japanese do to prevent another disaster?
8 Study Figure 1.10. What impacts of the earthquake and what progress are reported? ⇨

Review

● Volcanic eruptions and earthquakes occur mainly along and close to crustal plate margins.
● Eruptions and earthquakes are high energy natural events which can become disasters when they occur in populated areas.
● Prediction is still uncertain, but warning systems are improving and modern buildings are more earthquake-resistant.

2 The unquiet atmosphere

Main activities

Map and graph interpretation; information analysis.

Do you know?

? What causes changes and variations in: temperature; precipitation; humidity; air pressure; wind; cloud and sunshine amounts.

? What we mean by: depressions; anticyclones; fronts; air masses; trade winds; hurricanes.

? That the Inter-Tropical Convergence Zone (ITCZ) is a narrow zone of low pressure between the tropics where the North East and South East Trades meet.

Key ideas

● Weather conditions are short-term variations around long-term climatic averages.
● In any region, weather patterns vary from year to year, and so vary from long-term averages.
● Long-term climatic averages may be of little use in predicting weather conditions.
● Wide variations from long-term averages may cause problems for people.
● Extreme **meteorological** events have severe impacts upon human activities.

Our protective blanket

The atmosphere is the blanket of air wrapped around the surface of the earth. This blanket is a huge store for two things on which all living organisms depend: warmth and water. We adapt our lives to the temperature and moisture conditions around us. These conditions change constantly and affect our lives: during a day; from day to day; from one month to another; from year to year; and of course, from place to place (Figure 2.1).

Canada

Many Canadian temperature records were set. On June 18, Thunder Bay, in southern Ontario, recorded an all-time high of 39°C (102°F). During July, the heat wave that killed hundreds of people in Chicago, moved into Ontario on the 14th, bringing extreme heat and humidity. The impact was especially severe for the poultry industry, with ½ million chickens dying between the 14th and 17th.

China

June rainfall totalled more than 400mm (twice the normal) south of the Yangtze River valley. Flooding caused severe damage throughout the Yangtze basin in July, destroying over 2 million acres of rice land. Damage cost £12 billion, and 1600 people died.

Figure 2.1: Weather in two regions, June–July 1995

We call these short-term variations the 'weather'. However, every region has its own long-term patterns and rhythms, called 'climate'. We describe the climate of a region in terms of averages from records kept over many years. Weather conditions in any particular day, season or year will vary from the long-term averages of climate.

It is important to understand that we need to know not only the climate of a region, but also what variations from these average conditions we can expect. We need to know how reliable the climate is, and what kinds of extreme weather conditions might occur. It is from extreme and violent events such as floods, droughts, gales and heatwaves that we learn that the atmosphere can be a threat as well as a support to life on earth (Figure 2.2).

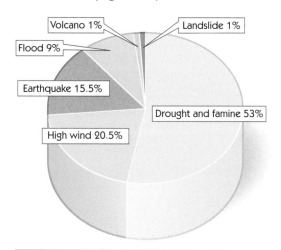

Volcano 1%   Landslide 1%
Flood 9%
Earthquake 15.5%
Drought and famine 53%
High wind 20.5%

Figure 2.2: Average percentages of people killed since 1969 through natural disasters

The first case study uses the Indian subcontinent to ask: 'Are climatic averages reliable and useful?'. In the second case study, we ask: 'What effects do extreme events have upon people's lives?' by following a hurricane as it hits South Florida, USA.

▼ Questions

Look again at the two regional reports in Figure 2.1.
1 In what ways did the weather during June and July 1995 vary from the normal climatic conditions of these months?
2 How did the weather extremes affect human lives and activities?

CASE STUDY: Monsoon rhythms of the Indian subcontinent

There is a popular saying in Britain: 'We don't have climate, only weather.' In Montana, USA, they tell you, 'If you don't like the weather now, just wait five minutes!' The idea behind these sayings is that some places have very unreliable and changeable conditions.

In other parts of the world, seasonal climatic rhythms seem to be more reliable and predictable. This regularity tends to occur where each season is dominated by a single type of air, or air mass. The best-known example is the monsoon climate of the Indian subcontinent. Figure 2.3 shows that the year has a wet season and a dry season, with the dry season being divided into a cool period and a hot period.

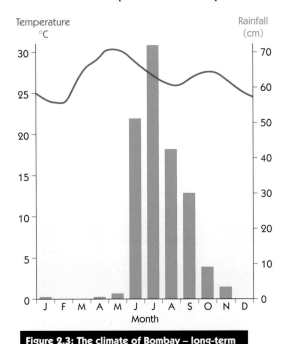

Figure 2.3: The climate of Bombay – long-term averages of temperature and rainfall

However, the Indian subcontinent covers a huge area (Figure 2.4). So, the materials in this case study help you to answer these key questions:
- Is the seasonal rhythm the same over the whole subcontinent?
- How reliable is the monsoon?
- What causes the monsoon climate?
- What impact does the monsoon have on the lives of the people?

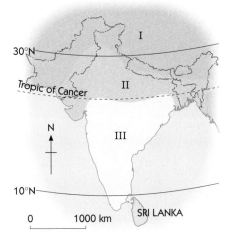

The Indian subcontinent is made up of three main countries: Bangladesh (pop. 118 million); India (920 million); Pakistan (126 million). In addition there is the island nation of Sri Lanka to the south and the mountain kingdoms of Afghanistan, Nepal and Bhutan along the northern rim.

Figure 2.4: Regions of the Indian subcontinent

I Northern mountain ranges

These include the Himalayas and Mount Everest, the world's highest mountain. They run in a great arc for more than 3000 kilometres and form a barrier between the subcontinent and the rest of Asia.

II The valleys of the Indus and Ganges–Brahmaputra rivers

The great rivers are fed by snowmelt in the mountain headwaters. This keeps them flowing all year, and provides irrigation and domestic water for millions of people. These broad, flat valleys may be seasonally flooded.

III The Deccan Plateau

The highest area is in the Ghats mountains along the western edge. It slopes steadily eastwards and is crossed by several large rivers.

Is the seasonal rhythm the same over the whole subcontinent?

The two maps of Figure 2.5 help us to answer this question. For example, Map A shows that if you live in Cochin, you expect the rains to arrive towards the end of May. However, if you live in Karachi the rains are likely to begin over a month later.

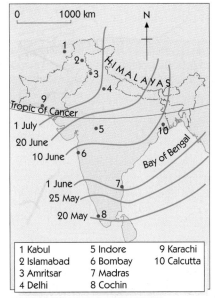

1 Kabul	5 Indore	9 Karachi
2 Islamabad	6 Bombay	10 Calcutta
3 Amritsar	7 Madras	
4 Delhi	8 Cochin	

A   The advance of the rains

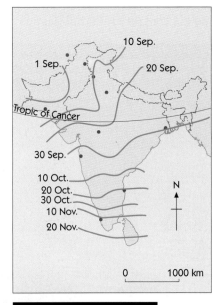

B   The retreat of the rains

Figure 2.5: The rainy season across the Indian subcontinent

Look at Figure 2.5.

1 Give the approximate dates on which the monsoon rains arrive in these cities:
   a   Bombay;
   b   Calcutta;
   c   Delhi;
   d   Karachi;
   e   Islamabad.

2 Use Map A to support this statement: 'The summer monsoon rains move steadily north and west across the Indian subcontinent.' ➡

3 a   Measure the straight-line distance between Cochin and Karachi.
   b   Approximately how many days does it take for the monsoon rains to move north from Cochin to Karachi?
   c   What is the average distance the monsoon rains move northwards each day?

4 Look at Map B.
   a   Estimate the dates on which the rains end in the five cities named in Question 1 above.
   b   What is the approximate length of the rainy season in each of the five cities?

5 Are the following statements accurate? (Use the maps and your answers to the earlier questions to support your answer.)
   a   'The monsoon rains retreat south and east across the subcontinent during September and October.'
   b   'The farther north you travel across the Indian subcontinent, the shorter is the monsoon rainy season.'

How reliable is the monsoon?

A climate is reliable if we can expect only small variations from year to year. In such climates, the weather is predictable. Important elements we can use to test the reliability of the Indian monsoon climate are: an increase in temperature during the dry season, and a fall in temperature during the wet season; the date of arrival of the rains; the rainfall totals at any particular place. Figures 2.6 and 2.8 contain useful information about these elements.

500 DEAD FROM SUNSTROKE

PRE-MONSOON HEAT caused hundreds of deaths in India and Pakistan during May and June for the second year running. Temperatures rose as high as 50°C (122°F). The monsoon rains started in southern India around June 8, about a week late. By the time the first rains finally began to cool northern India around June 17, more than 500 people had died from sunstroke. The monsoon's slow advance north caused planting delays, but most of India and Pakistan had normal or above-normal rainfall in July and August. This resulted in above-average seasonal totals and good crops.

As is often the case, the plentiful monsoon rains caused floods which took hundreds of lives, and caused severe local crop damage. In Pakistan, flooding from heavy rains late in July and early August killed 451 people. July floods in Bangladesh killed 260 people and affected 25 million others. Further floods in October affected 8 million people and killed 325. Floods and landslides in September in Nepal killed 183 people.

Figure 2.6: Report of the 1995 Indian summer monsoon

Use Figure 2.6, which summarises the 1995 summer. (An atlas will help you to locate the places mentioned.)

6 Did temperatures become very high towards the end of the dry season?

7 Did the monsoon rains arrive on their usual dates?

8 Were the rainfall totals 'normal'?

9 It is dangerous to use the information of only one year, but does the 1995 summer support the idea that the Indian monsoon climate is reliable?

10 Why do you think intense tropical rainstorms, although normal, lead to flooding?

11 Why does the flooding have such serious effects upon people's lives across the Indian subcontinent? (Figure 2.7 may help you.)

Figure 2.7: Water – a blessing and a threat. Intensive agriculture is possible on this floodplain because of water for irrigation from the river. On the other hand, heavy monsoon rains on the surrounding hills can result in serious flooding of this densely populated farmland.

We can take a closer look by studying the figures for particular places. The graphs and tables of Figure 2.8 are for the cities of Amritsar (A), in the Indo–Gangetic Plain of northern India, and Indore (B), on the Deccan Plateau. The bar graphs for the mean monthly rainfall totals in Amritsar show the typical monsoon climatic rhythm. The rains arrive in June and are retreating southwards in September. The coloured markers give the monthly rainfall totals for the 1995 and 1996 summers. Both years were wetter than average, but in each year the rains arrived in a quite different pattern. We can see, too, that in neither summer did any month bring an 'average' rainfall. The line graphs show the climatic mean monthly temperatures and the actual monthly means for the 1995 and 1996 summers.

▼ Questions

Look at Figure 2.8.

12 Use the figures for Indore (B) to construct graphs similar to those for Amritsar (A).

13 Calculate the following June–September rainfall totals for Amritsar and Indore: (a) long-term climatic mean; (b) 1995; (c) 1996; (d) the difference between each year's total and the mean.

14 Did the 1995 and 1996 temperatures follow (a) the seasonal trend, (b) the monthly means?

15 Some schools exchange information with schools in other countries. As a High School student in Amritsar, write a brief report for a school in Britain, describing the 1995 and 1996 summer monsoon seasons. ✐

16 Use the information from Figures 2.5–2.8 to make two lists:
● Evidence which supports the statement that the Indian monsoon climate is reliable.
● Evidence which indicates that the Indian monsoon climate is unreliable.

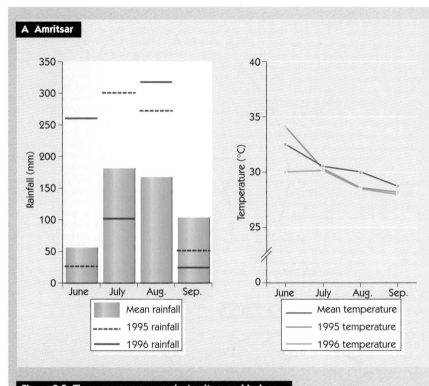

A Amritsar

B Indore

Rainfall (mm)

	Mean	1995	1996
June	68	40	143
July	285	487	643
August	290	205	221
September	221	162	172

Temperature (°C)

	Mean	1995	1996
June	30.2	31.0	28.8
July	26.3	27.3	27.7
August	25.0	26.2	25.2
September	25.1	26.8	26.2

Figure 2.8: The summer monsoon in Amritsar and Indore

What causes the Indian monsoon climate?

We can answer this question in three sentences:
● During the winter, a dry continental **air mass** covers the subcontinent.
● During the summer, a warm, moist tropical maritime air mass dominates.
● The monsoon rains arrive when the tropical maritime air takes over from the continental air.

But this answer does *not* explain what causes the air masses to move. We can follow the explanation by starting with the position of the overhead sun (Figure 2.9). In the northern hemisphere winter the sun is overhead south of the equator. The heating caused by the overhead sun creates low air pressures. The two main tropical wind systems, the North East and South East Trades, are drawn into this low pressure region. They meet in the **Inter-Tropical Convergence Zone** (ITCZ), also known as the Equatorial Trough. By December, dry northerly winds from the high pressure of northern Asia blow across much of the Indian subcontinent (Figure 2.10A). This northerly airstream brings dry conditions.

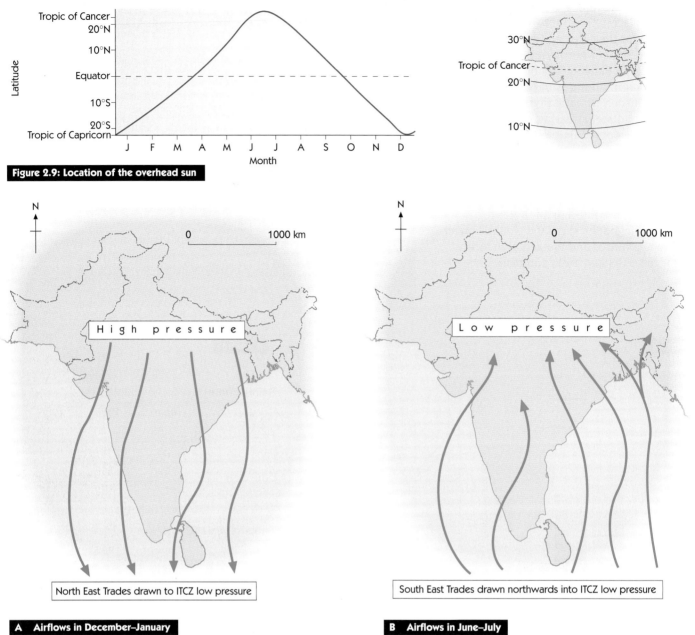

Figure 2.9: Location of the overhead sun

A   Airflows in December–January

North East Trades drawn to ITCZ low pressure

B   Airflows in June–July

South East Trades drawn northwards into ITCZ low pressure

Figure 2.10: Indian subcontinent: general seasonal airflow

In April and May, the overhead sun, followed by the ITCZ of low pressure, moves north of the equator, and the land becomes hotter. As the ITCZ pushes north through June, it draws the warm, moist tropical maritime air of the South East Trades with it. This causes the onset of the summer rains (Figure 2.10B). Low pressure over the hot interior of Pakistan and central India helps the rains to continue through August.

By September the overhead sun has retreated southwards, followed by the ITCZ. Once again the dry continental air of the North East Trades begins to move south and the wet season ends.

▼ **Questions**

Use Figures 2.5 and 2.9.

17 When does the overhead sun, moving north, reach (a) Cochin; (b) Calcutta?

18 When does the overhead sun, moving south after the summer solstice, pass over (a) Calcutta; (b) Cochin?

19 Use your answers to the two questions above, and the maps in Figure 2.5 and 2.10, to explain the timing and length of the summer monsoon rains in Calcutta. (Remember, the ITCZ arrives about two weeks after the date of the overhead sun at a particular place). ➡

Key ideas

● Hurricanes are intense tropical storms which move across great distances.
● Some regions are more affected by hurricanes than others.

Do you know?

? A hurricane is an extreme form of low pressure system or depression.
? In the northern hemisphere, winds blow anticlockwise around a depression.
? Heated air and warm ocean water combine to give tropical storms, including hurricanes, their immense energy.

Hurricane 'Andrew'

At 4.30 a.m. on Monday 24 August 1992, **Hurricane** 'Andrew' hit the east coast of Florida south of Miami. By 8.00 a.m. it was gone, but the effects were enormous (Figure 2.11). The report tells us two useful things:
● The damage was especially great because the storm crossed a large urban area.
● The hurricane was not a surprise.

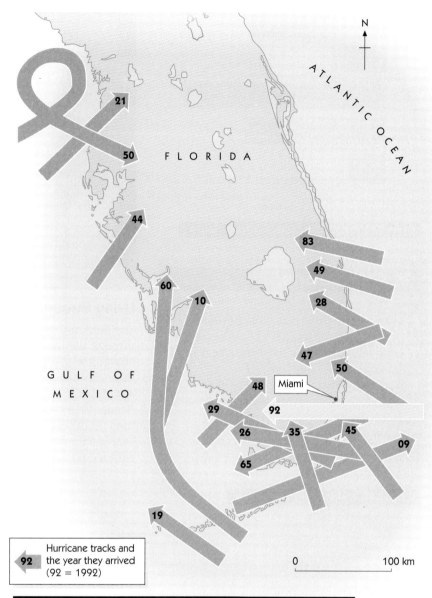

Hurricane tracks and the year they arrived (92 = 1992)

Figure 2.12: South Florida: Hurricanes of the twentieth century (to 1992)

THE HURRICANE THAT CHANGED EVERYTHING

This was the Big One. The hurricane experts have been worrying about it for years: a storm with monster winds of over 150 miles [240 kilometres] an hour slamming into a major urban area. Casualties were surprisingly light: no more than 20 killed directly by the storm. But in terms of property destruction, Hurricane 'Andrew' was the worst natural disaster ever to hit the United States. It changed the face of South Florida forever. 'Andrew' destroyed $20 billion in property, demolished 25,000 homes and seriously damaged another 50,000. About 175,000 people were left homeless.

Figure 2.11: By J. Doschner of the Miami Herald

▼ Questions

Study Figure 2.12.

1 How many hurricanes have hit South Florida this century?

2 List the years in which the hurricanes occurred.

3 What is the longest time gap between hurricanes?

4 When 'Andrew' arrived, how long had it been since the last hurricane?

5 From which direction do most of the hurricanes arrive?

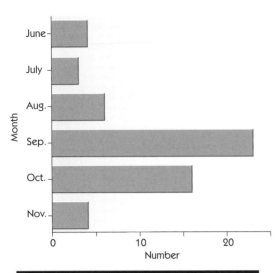

Figure 2.13: The hurricane season in South Florida

Figure 2.14: Damage caused by Hurricane 'Andrew'

▼ Questions

Study Figure 2.13.

6 Which month is the peak of the hurricane season in South Florida?

7 How does 'Andrew' fit into the seasonal pattern of hurricanes?

8 Use your answers to these questions to explain, in not more than two sentences, why Hurricane 'Andrew' came as no great surprise to the people of South Florida.

Living through 'Andrew'

The hurricane passed directly through the towns south of Miami itself. Winds reached more than 255 kilometres per hour, and ripped many homes apart (Figure 2.14). Although more than 30,000 people had been evacuated, many stayed – and suffered (Figure 2.15).

▼ Questions

Study Figure 2.15.

9 From which direction were the winds blowing when the hurricane approached Juan's house?

10 Why was there quiet for a few minutes during the hurricane?

11 From which direction were the winds blowing as the hurricane moved away from Juan's house?

12 Describe the movement of winds within a hurricane.

13 What words does Juan use to describe what was happening?

Review

● The monsoon of the Indian subcontinent advances northwards during summer and retreats southwards during the autumn, following the movement of the ITCZ.

● The monsoon climate has a well-developed seasonal rhythm, but there are wide variations from year to year. These variations can affect people's lives.

● Hurricanes are violent tropical storms. They follow well-defined paths and so are hazards in certain regions such as Florida and the Caribbean.

● Hurricane forecasting is now efficient, but impacts can still be severe.

Figure 2.15: 'Andrew' visits Juan's house

City of Miami

Juan's house

Hurricane eye

Hurricane path

Everglades National Park

N

0   20 km

Florida Keys

The hurricane at 4.00 a.m.

Wind direction (anticlockwise)

Juan's story

From midnight, the wind and rain got worse. By 3 o'clock the wind was screeching and hammering on the north side of the house. By 4.30, the shaking and howling were frightening. Then suddenly, everything went quiet. I knew the 'eye' of the storm was over us. Then – BANG – after about 20 minutes the wind hammered into the house from the south. By 8 o'clock it was still raining but the wind was less strong. All the roof of the house had gone.

3 Managing ecosystems

Figure 3.1: Without a home, this bison will die. Bison will only survive if the grass and woodland habitat, on which they depend, survives.

Main activity

Making decisions about **ecosystem** conservation strategies.

Key ideas

● Conservation involves maintaining the structure and functions of an ecosystem.
● All ecosystems change and adjust over time.
● There may be conflicts between economic and conservation priorities.
● Natural ecosystems are becoming increasingly rare.
● Setting up protected areas can help to conserve ecosystems and wildlife.
● Wildlife species need habitats to live in. Without these 'homes', creatures die out.
● Areas set up to protect wildlife need careful management.

Do you know?

❓ How food chains and **trophic levels** play their part in making ecosystems work.
❓ That an ecosystem has a structure, a way of working (function) and a species composition.
❓ Where **wetland** ecosystems are found.
❓ The special characteristics of wetland ecosystems and the way they work.
❓ Why natural wetlands are disappearing rapidly, all over the world.

Putting wildlife first

An increasing number of countries are setting up special areas to protect ecosystems and wildlife. This is happening for two main reasons:
● Humans are using more and more of the world's resources.
● People are realising how precious wildlife and natural ecosystems are, and want to conserve them.

The main purpose of these parks, reserves and refuges is to conserve the **habitat** and the **species** which depend on this habitat (Figure 3.1).

A second purpose is to allow visitors to learn about, enjoy and care for these special places. In the USA the government has created the National Wildlife Refuge System, with refuges in every one of the 50 states (Figure 3.2).

In many wildlife refuges the ecosystems are no longer 'natural'. Wetland ecosystems are good examples. Marshlands, floodplains and deltas often make fertile farmland when they are drained and floods controlled. Throughout the world, wetlands are threatened. There are two useful conservation approaches:
● Carefully conserve remnants of the original environment, e.g. the Nature Reserve at Wicken Fen, Cambridgeshire. Here you can walk through the reed fen environment.

● Restore natural conditions and habitats, and manage them to support the traditional wildlife species. The example of the Bosque del Apache National Wildlife Refuge, USA, shows how this works.

Restoration also involves replacing some missing pieces of ecosystem, so that it can function efficiently. In Yellowstone National Park this has meant re-introducing the wolf to this environment. You will learn, as you study the materials, that not everyone agrees with this way of conserving an ecosystem.

■ Where wildlife comes naturally!

Welcome to your national wildlife refuges. Managed by the US Fish and Wildlife Service, this diverse System of 500+ refuges encompassing over 92 million acres [37 million hectares] of lands and waters spans the continent from Alaska's Arctic tundra to the tropical forests in Florida; from the secluded atolls of Hawaii to the moose-trodden bogs of Maine.

National wildlife refuges were established for many different purposes. Most were established to protect and enhance wetlands for the conservation of migratory birds; some were established to provide habitat for the Nation's endangered species. Within refuge habitats exist a diversity of plants and animals that have their own special requirements for survival.

National wildlife refuges protect virtually every type of habitat – food, water, cover, and space – for the survival of fish and wildlife. Refuges provide habitat for over 200 endangered and threatened species as well as hundreds of other birds, mammals, reptiles, amphibians, fish, and plants. Over 60 refuges have been acquired specifically to protect endangered species.

Figure 3.2

A wetland revived

Most of the Bosque del Apache National Wildlife Refuge (NWR) is a wetland. It spreads across 23,000 hectares of the Rio Grande floodplain in south-central New Mexico (Figure 3.3).

It was set up in 1939 'as a refuge and breeding grounds for migratory birds and other wildlife'. Today at least 100,000 visitors come each year. Cranes and geese are the main attraction, but 329 species of bird have been observed in the refuge.

Yet there is something very special about this refuge, as this brief conversation suggests:

Tourist: 'Gee, it's great that there are still some natural places for all these birds.'

Refuge manager: 'Well, ma'am, it may look natural, but it sure isn't!'

The role of the floodplain ecosystem

The river and its floodplain support two types of bird populations: resident species who stay all year, and migratory species who stay for a season or who rest and feed before flying on. This is a vital piece of one of the great **flyways** running north–south across North America. The migrating birds follow the Rio Grande valley south in the autumn and return north in the spring. For thousands of years, these birds have relied on the floodplain wetlands for food, drink and shelter. The Bosque del Apache has been an important 'stopover' or 'winter home' for thousands of birds, especially cranes, ducks and geese. There are also many permanent residents.

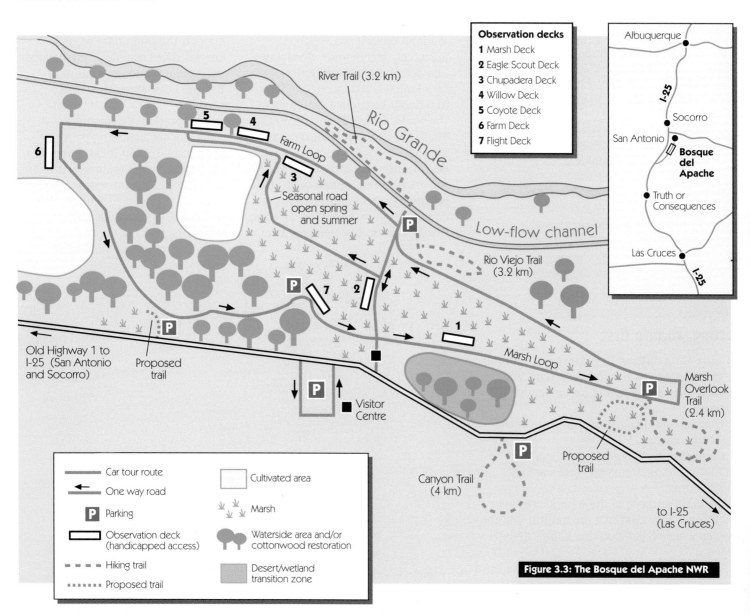

Figure 3.3: The Bosque del Apache NWR

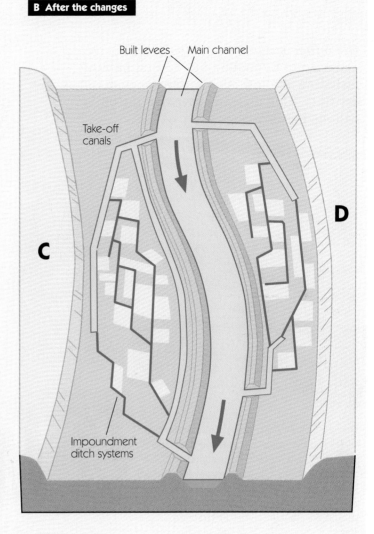

A Before the changes

Natural levees   Main channel

A

B

Ponds, marsh
and reeds

← Floodplain 3 km wide →

B After the changes

Built levees   Main channel

Take-off
canals

C

D

Impoundment
ditch systems

Features:

◆ **Meandering river**

◆ **Ponds and marshes**

◆ **Seasonal flooding
(in spring and summer)**

◆ **Marsh and woodland
vegetation**

◆ **Low natural levees**

◆ **High water-table**

Features:

◆ **Straightened river channel**

◆ **Canals and ditches
across floodplain**

◆ **No seasonal floods**

◆ **Alfalfa and maize crops**

◆ **Higher built levees**

◆ **Lower water-table**

Figure 3.4: Changes to the Rio Grande floodplain

So what happened?

Figure 3.4 shows how humans have transformed much of the Rio Grande floodplain. As drainage, farming and flood control expanded, the wetlands disappeared. The flyway was being wiped out. Imagine the impact for motorists of closing all the motorway cafes and petrol stations between London and Edinburgh!

▼ Questions

1 What is meant by a 'flyway'?
2 Look at Figure 3.4A:
   a Draw a labelled cross-section along line A–B.
   b Describe the landscape of the natural ecosystem.
   c Explain how this environment gave food, water and shelter to birds.
3 Look at Figure 3.4B. Draw a labelled cross-section along line C–D.
4 What have been the main environmental changes from the natural situation?
5 Explain why this modern landscape is a poor habitat for many bird species. ➡

The refuge manager explains:

The natural floodplain has several habitats, including shallow open water, soggy marshes and dry flats. This diversity satisfied the birds' various needs.

So, what we try to do is to copy or simulate nature. We take water from the Rio Grande and lead it through the refuge via canals and ditches (Figure 3.5). Each year we have controlled floods into parts of the refuge. These three pictures show you:

We have divided the refuge into enclosures called **impoundments**, surrounded by low embankments. In this photo, two Canada geese stand on one of the banks. This year the water-table in the impoundment beyond is being kept low enough for rich marsh vegetation to grow. This gives excellent food and shelter for the birds. Water flow and water levels are controlled by opening and shutting sluice gates like the one here.

We flooded this impoundment last year to give open water and fish. About 17,000 sandhill cranes and at least 30,000 snow geese spend their winters here. These visitors in April are watching the last of the geese before they fly north to Canada. The cranes have already left for Idaho. The open sluice gate is draining an impoundment away to the right, which we want as dry grassland this summer. The water runs through a culvert to a canal.

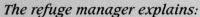

Figure 3.5

The result is as near to a natural landscape as we can manage. You can see the route of the straightened Rio Grande in the distance as a dark line of trees along the high levee. The floodplain is a mixture of water, marsh and grassland – just as it should be! Each year, too, it changes – just as it should do! You can see how dry the climate is and so how vital the water is for the birds and other creatures.

Figure 3.6

Figure 3.7: The managed ecosystem today

One more problem

The refuge is surrounded by farmlands. The birds are not aware that their refuge has boundaries, so fly off to 'raid' the farmers' fields. Not surprisingly, this makes the farmers angry. A large flock of cranes or geese can devour several hectares of maize or wheat in a single night.

After long arguments, the refuge managers have worked out a deal with the farmers. The farmers are allowed to plough and plant about 700 hectares inside the refuge (look at the 'cultivated area' symbol on Figure 3.3). They grow maize and alfalfa, then harvest the alfalfa for their own use as hay, leaving the maize as winter feed for the birds. The refuge staff also grow some maize, clover and native plants. As a result, the birds do not need to leave the refuge so much for food.

▼ Questions

6 Why did the refuge manager say to the tourist that the Bosque environment is not 'natural'?

7 Make two lists:
● Ways in which the Bosque del Apache ecosystem is similar to the 'natural' one.
● Ways in which it is different from the 'natural' one.

8 Describe and explain how ecosystem conservation can succeed by simulating (copying) natural processes.➡

CASE STUDY: The wolf in the Yellowstone ecosystem

Main activity

Decision making.

The issues

Conservation is one of the main reasons why National Parks are set up. Often this means the conservation of precious ecosystems. However, park managers have to answer some awkward questions, for example:
● Should they restore an ecosystem that has been affected by human activities?
● What type of ecosystem do the large numbers of visitors want to enjoy?
● Will the conservation policy annoy the people who live and work around the park?

This case study is about the place of one species – the wolf – in the ecosystem of Yellowstone National Park, Wyoming, USA (Figure 3.8). This example illustrates how difficult conserving an ecosystem can be.

Figure 3.9: The Yellowstone environment

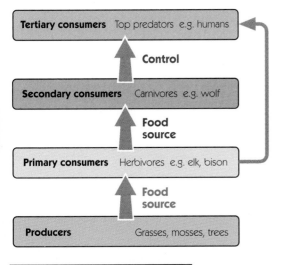

Figure 3.8: A Yellowstone food chain

Tertiary consumers Top predators e.g. humans

↑ Control

Secondary consumers Carnivores e.g. wolf

↑ Food source

Primary consumers Herbivores e.g. elk, bison

↑ Food source

Producers Grasses, mosses, trees

FACTFILE: Yellowstone National Park

The world's first National Park, established in 1872.

Area	920,000 hectares
Environment	High plateaus, crossed by mountain ridges (Figure 3.9)
Climate	Warm summers with occasional rainstorms. Severe winters, with heavy snow cover, October–March.
Ecosystems	A rich variety of forests, grass meadows, wetlands, rivers and lakes supports many animals, including bear, bison, elk and wolf. The food chain in Figure 3.8 shows how this fits together, including the place of humans.

Figure 3.10: Grey wolf at stream

The park at work

The second main purpose of National Parks is to provide attractions for visitors. Around 3 million visitors come to Yellowstone each year. Most arrive between May and September, although the popularity of snowmobiles means more are using the park during the winter. A 1994 visitor survey found that the three main reasons people come are: 'to view the wildlife' (93% of all visitors); 'to see the thermal features', that is the **geysers**, etc. (85%); 'to take photographs of the scenery and animals' (83%). The 'Top Two' species which attract people are grizzly bears and bison, which are now found in very few parts of the USA (Figure 3.11). The elk herds, too, are popular.

In 1988, disastrous fires burned two-thirds of the forests. This fire damage, and the regrowth of young trees as the ecosystem recovers, has become a popular attraction. Visitors are excited, too, about the chance to hear, and possibly see, a wolf.

Before 1860: Wolves are the top **predator** in the natural ecosystem. They help to keep the ecosystem in balance by controlling herbivore numbers.

From 1860: Cattle ranching and sheep rearing spread through Wyoming and Montana. Wolves are trapped and shot because they kill calves and lambs.

1872: Yellowstone National Park set up. No cattle or sheep grazing within the park. No hunting except for the wolf.

1923: The last wolf in Yellowstone is killed.

From 1920s: No wolves in the park. With no wolves and no hunting, the ecosystem is out of balance – elk and bison numbers grow rapidly.

From 1980: Park managers realise that meadows are being overgrazed and young trees eaten. There are too many elk and bison. Hunting is still banned so scientists work out how wolves can be brought back.

Winter 1994: 15 wolves from similar habitats in Canada are released. This project is supported by environmentalists and tourists, but opposed by ranchers (Figure 3.12).

Plan for 2000: About 100 wolves in ten packs.

The park managers are keen to bring the wolves back for two reasons. First, it will complete the ecosystem once more. Second, the wolves will help to control herbivore numbers and conserve the grasses and trees.

Figure 3.11: Crowds gather wherever elk, bison and bears appear near the one road through the park

Park Ranger

It is our job to restore things to a natural state. This means making the Yellowstone ecosystem as complete as we can. Things were different in the old days. We actually helped to get rid of the wolves. We thought they were a dangerous pest. Now we understand more about how ecosystems work. We want the wolf back because this is the top predator in the natural ecosystem. It helps control the numbers of herbivores such as elk and bison. Also, tourists want to hear a wolf howl and, if possible, to see one.

Tourist

I'm not sure really. The wolf is pretty scary. But so are grizzly bears, and they are protected in the park. People come from all over to see the bears, the bison and the elk. Now, to be here and hope to see or hear a wolf is exciting. It's what these wild places are all about. The ranchers are all upset about wolves killing their calves and lambs. But how many can a few wolves kill? But they may be dangerous in a park where there are so many people. On the other hand, the Wyoming Tourist Board folk reckon the wolf will be worth another $3 million a year in extra tourist spending.

Rancher

The wolf is a dangerous pest. A number of years ago we wiped them out in this part of the country. Now some 'greenies' and the park managers have brought them back. It's OK if the wolves stay inside the park, where we don't have our stock. But wolves cover large areas and they'll roam far beyond the park. Just a month ago, a friend of mine captured a wolf over 100 miles [160 kilometres] from the park. Wolves don't just kill to eat, you know. These cattle are my living, and in one night a single wolf took six of my calves.

Environmentalist

We have fought for years to get the wolf back. Humans have taken up so much of the planet – surely we have to leave some space for other creatures? Wolves have a right to live, but they can survive only if we let them. Isn't this what National Parks are about? They are protected areas where ecosystems can work in a natural way. And where we have the chance to enjoy them. There will be only around one hundred wolves in Yellowstone and there is a large elk and bison population. So, there's plenty of food within the park. And elk numbers are too high anyway.

Figure 3.12: Four contrasting opinions about the return of the wolf

▼ Questions

1 Describe briefly the part the wolf plays in the natural ecosystem of Yellowstone.
2 Why were wolves removed from the ecosystem?
3 What happened to the ecosystem once the two predators, (a) wolves and (b) human hunters, were removed?
4 Make two lists:
 ● Reasons for opposing the return of the wolf.
 ● Reasons for supporting the return of the wolf.
5 Decide which side you support, and write a brief report arguing your case.

Review

● Conservation of wildlife today may mean recreating natural conditions. This aims to provide a sustainable habitat for the wildlife, as in the Bosque del Apache.
● Conserving an ecosystem means maintaining a balance between its various parts. This is not easy when differing demands are made on the ecosystem.
● Providing opportunities for visitor enjoyment and education is an important part of ecosystem management, as both Bosque del Apache and Yellowstone illustrate.

4 Resources and sustainability

● To be **sustainable**, use of a **renewable resource** must not be greater than the productive capacity of that resource.
● Sustainable resource management has to balance conservation and development needs.
● Local communities have to be convinced of the benefits of conservation, and to have some control over resource conservation.

Main activity

Evaluating resource management strategies.

Introduction

We use the old saying: 'Oh, there's plenty more fish in the sea!' when we mean 'there is plenty more where that came from'. But countries all over the world are finding that this is not true. Modern fishing fleets have got bigger and gone 'high tech' to supply our growing demand (Figure 4.1).

The result is that at least 70% of the world's sea fisheries show signs of overfishing. Decline of fish stocks has become a global problem (Figure 4.2).

Figure 4.1: Factory ship handling fish

GOING, GOING, GONE: THE COD OF NEWFOUNDLAND

For hundreds of years the people of coastal Newfoundland have enjoyed some of the richest fishing grounds in the world. The sea here teems with plankton, whales, seals, fish, and the fishing villages have grown used to the annual harvest of cod. But in recent years the fishermen, with their increasingly efficient and mechanised methods, have been taking out more than nature can put back. The result: declining fish stocks.

Finally, in 1992, the nightmare happened: commercial cod fishing was banned in Newfoundland. In 1993 the ban was extended to cover the whole of eastern Canada.

Figure 4.2

The world fish catch peaked in 1989, and since then has been declining. Near to home, Britain's main source of fish, the North Sea, is sending us the same message (Figure 4.3).

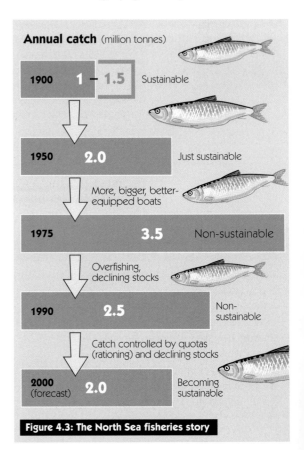

Annual catch (million tonnes)

1900	1 – 1.5	Sustainable
1950	2.0	Just sustainable
		More, bigger, better-equipped boats
1975	3.5	Non-sustainable
		Overfishing, declining stocks
1990	2.5	Non-sustainable
		Catch controlled by quotas (rationing) and declining stocks
2000 (forecast)	2.0	Becoming sustainable

Figure 4.3: The North Sea fisheries story

? How an ecosystem works as a collection of living organisms and non-living components.
? That a number of food chains and food webs are found within an ecosystem.
? What we mean by the productive capacity of an ecosystem.
? That conservation means managing an ecosystem so that its productive capacity is sustained.
? Which countries have the largest ocean fishing fleets and what they catch.

▼ Questions

1 Look at Figure 4.2.
  a What has caused the decline in fish stocks?
  b Why do you think the Canadian government has banned commercial fishing, and what effect do they think the ban should have?
  c What may happen to the people of the fishing villages?
2 Use the example of Figure 4.4 to explain what we mean by 'sustainable' and 'non-sustainable'.

To be sustainable, catches must be less than the weight of young fish which replace those caught. This is the **productive capacity** of the North Sea (Figure 4.4).

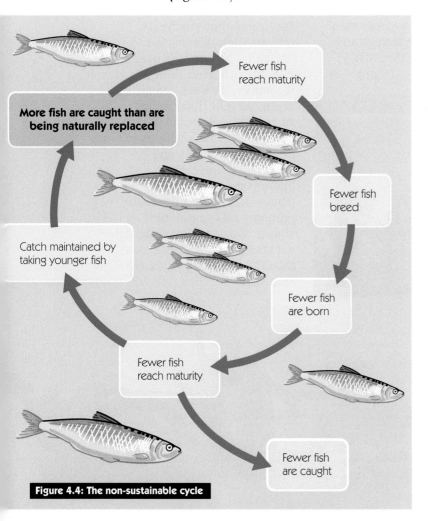

More fish are caught than are being naturally replaced

Fewer fish reach maturity

Fewer fish breed

Fewer fish are born

Fewer fish reach maturity

Catch maintained by taking younger fish

Fewer fish are caught

Figure 4.4: The non-sustainable cycle

Looking for ways to solve the problem

The answer to declining fish stocks seems easy: Catch fewer fish! But this answer raises more questions, such as, 'How do we make this happen?' and 'By how much must we reduce the catch?' As the list in Figure 4.5 shows, there are several ways to control fish catches.

Policy	Description
Exclusive fishing	A single country has the rights to fish a certain area of the sea. The boundaries of this area may be decided by the country itself, or by international agreement.
Catch limits	A limit is set to the catch of certain species within an area. This limit may be set by an individual country or agreed by countries whose boats fish the area.
Quotas	A form of rationing. The boats of each country which fishes an area are allowed an agreed proportion of the total catch.
Size limits	For each species, only fish above a certain size may be caught and kept. The aim is to conserve the stocks of younger fish.
Zoning	An area of ocean is divided into a set of zones. The fishing in each zone is controlled according to the fish stocks in that zone. For example, a zone may be closed for a period, but fishing continues in other zones.
Fleet limits	Limits are set to the number of boats and to their catch capacity. For example, one large, high-tech boat can catch far more than an older, smaller boat.
Equipment control	The fishing techniques are controlled. This is applied particularly to the size and type of nets used. For example, a larger mesh size allows smaller fish to escape.

Figure 4.5: Options for controlling fish catches

The problems lie in making them work. Here are some of the difficulties:

● Oceans are not 'owned' by individual countries. Beyond a coastal zone of 'territorial waters' where a country does have rights, the oceans are 'international waters'.

● Oceans cover huge areas, so how can we know if fishing boats are obeying the regulations?

● Who should make sure the regulations are working, and who should pay for this service?

● How good is our information about fish stocks? After all, fish move mysteriously through the oceans, so how do we count them? How much do we know about the way a species recovers from a disaster such as overfishing?

● Demand for fish is increasing, so prices rise and it is easy to understand why fishermen want to catch as many fish as they can.

● Not all governments support regulations and restrictions on their national fishing fleets.

▼ Questions

3 Choose *one* of the policies suggested in Figure 4.5.
   a   Describe how it can manage fishing and control fish stocks in an area of the ocean.
   b   Give reasons why it might be difficult to make the policy work.
4 An area of ocean is being overfished. Write a letter to a newspaper, proposing how the area could be managed for sustainable fishing. Your proposal will work best if you combine several of the individual policies given in Figure 4.5.

Harvesting the ocean in Alaska

Looking ahead

Alaska is the largest state in the USA, but has a population of less than 600,000. At least one-half live in the two main cities of Anchorage and Fairbanks. A majority of the other half are scattered along the coast, in villages and towns facing the Pacific Ocean such as Cordova (Figure 4.6).

Figure 4.6: Cordova, Alaska

Today, Alaska is a wealthy state, mainly because of the Prudhoe Bay oilfield of the North Slope (see Case Study: Arctic National Wildlife Refuge, pages 42–45). Tax money raised from the oil companies means that Alaskans pay no state income tax – every year they actually receive around $1000 each from the state government! But oil is a **non-renewable** resource. Within 30 years the oilfields may be exhausted. It is not surprising, therefore, that Alaska needs to look ahead and conserve its renewable resources. The two most important are fish and forests.

Fishing for life

For several thousand years, communities all along the Alaskan coastline have lived from the rich seas. These are the native Alaskans, consisting of a number of tribal groups such as the Aleuts and the Eyak. Their traditional way of life was based on fishing, e.g. salmon, halibut, herring, and hunting, e.g. seals and whales (Figure 4.7). This **subsistence economy** was **sustainable**. That is, the native Alaskans did not take out of the ocean more than the ecosystem produced each year.

Figure 4.7: Alaskan people butchering a whale

▼ Questions

1 Draw an outline map of Alaska (use an atlas to help you):
 a Draw in and label these lines of latitude: 55°N; 70°N; Arctic Circle.
 b Draw in and label these lines of longitude: 141°W; 168°W.
 c Measure the N–S and E–W distances across Alaska. Draw arrows along the margins of your map and label the arrows with the distances.

2 On the map:
 a Name these six cities and towns: Anchorage; Cordova; Fairbanks; Juneau; Seward; Valdez.
 b Name the following: Aleutian Islands; Bering Sea; Gulf of Alaska; Kodiak Island; Prince William Sound; Prudhoe Bay.
 c Draw in and name the North Pacific and Bering Sea ocean currents.

3 Define:
 a Renewable resource;
 b Non-renewable resource.

4 Name one renewable and one non-renewable resource found in Alaska.

Fishing for money

Today this has all changed. The North Pacific Ocean has been dangerously overfished and the numbers of several species are greatly reduced, e.g. salmon, halibut, whales (Figure 4.8). The fishing industry has become **non-sustainable** – more is being taken out of the ocean than the ecosystem is producing.

> *It's all caused by the huge growth in commercial fishing ...*

Problems for fish have come really since 1960. In Alaska there are more boats; bigger, faster boats; better equipped boats. Large onshore canneries and processing plants can take in far larger catches. But the real problems come from outside Alaska. Big factory ships come from Seattle – down in the main part of USA – and from Japan and even Norway. They fish with huge nets, or load up directly from the fishing boats and freeze and process the fish. The Japanese, especially, are a problem. Their huge trawl nets may be a kilometre long and simply sweep up everything. They strip the fish from wide areas.

> *... We've got to the situation where more fish are being taken out than are being produced. This is particularly true for the valuable species like salmon, herring and halibut.*

Figure 4.8: The overfishing issue, by Linda Scheider (fisheries research officer)

Conserving Alaska's fish stocks

Prince William Sound is one of Alaska's richest fishing grounds, especially for salmon. A fishing fleet of over 700 boats, based in three main ports, catches 15 to 30 million salmon a year (Figure 4.9). Prices vary, but the catch can be worth up to £30 million in a single summer. The Prince William Sound ecosystem and the fishing industry are still recovering from the massive Exxon Valdez oil spill disaster of 1989.

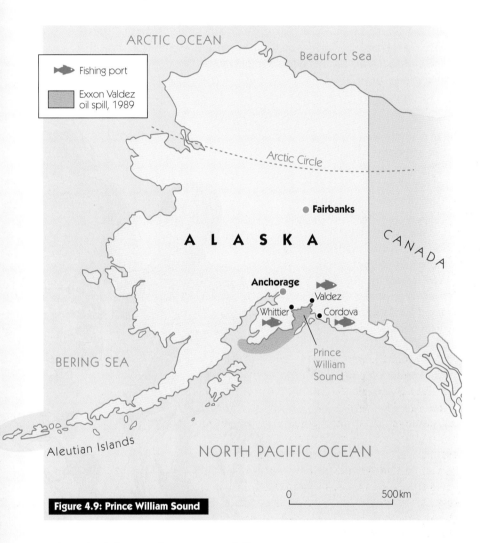

Figure 4.9: Prince William Sound

Today, the fishing industry is carefully controlled. Four people from the fishing town of Cordova explain how it works (Figures 4.10–4.14).

▼ Questions

Look at Figure 4.8.

5 What factors have made it possible for the commercial fishing industry to catch so many more fish?

6 Why is the scientist worried about threats from outside Alaska?

7 Use the Alaskan fishing example to define and explain what we mean by 'sustainable' and 'non-sustainable'.

I work for the Alaska Department of Environmental Conservation, known as ADEC. It's our job to study the life cycle of salmon and other fish. Salmon are very special fish. They are born in freshwater streams, often far inland. The young salmon, known as 'fry', swim to the sea. When they are strong enough, they disappear out into the North Pacific.

From two to four years later, they return to the coastal seas and to the same streams in which they were born. Once there, the females lay their eggs (called 'spawning'), and then die. It is on this return migration, or 'run', across the coastal waters that the fish are caught. One of our key jobs at ADEC is to estimate how many salmon are reaching their spawning streams. So, we have counting stations on the main streams. We need to know that enough salmon are spawning for fish stocks to be maintained.

I'm with the Alaska Department of Fish and Game – the ADFG. It's our job to decide how many salmon the fishing fleet is allowed to catch. First of all, ADEC tells us how many fish need to reach the various spawning streams for salmon stocks to be maintained. The streams are spread along hundreds of miles of coast, and the Sound is huge. So we have divided it into 11 management zones. Look at the map (Figure 4.14A).

We must let certain numbers escape through each zone. We call this the 'escapement run'. During the summer we track the salmon runs by using ship and aircraft radar and sonar. Only when the fish runs in a particular zone are large enough, do we allow fishing in that zone. Even then, to control the total catch, we set a time limit. We broadcast this information, and it is called 'declaring an opener'. Figure 4.14B is an example.

We also control the total number of boats. All fishing vessels must be licensed and we are offering very few new licenses. So, if anyone wants to buy an existing license, it is expensive – up to $90,000 in 1994.

The salmon runs last from end-May till September. The busiest time is in July and August. These days, we can only fish when the Fish and Game people say so. They also tell us what type of net mesh we can use. It can get frustrating, but we agree with the controls really. All the boats and modern equipment could wipe out the escapement fish some years.

A bigger problem for us is the way prices for salmon go up and down. Like most people, we sell our catch to the canneries in Cordova. When an 'opener' is declared, we need to know the price we're likely to get. Only then can we decide whether it is worth the expense of sailing out to the open zone for perhaps 12 hours' fishing. For example, for several years after the Exxon Valdez oil spill in 1989, people weren't buying Prince William Sound salmon. Prices fell, canneries closed, and we could do little fishing. It was hard, as we have a large loan on the boat.

During the 1980s, demand for salmon was rising. But most of the fishermen and the cannery owners could see that the catch had to be restricted. The answer has been – increase the number of salmon in the ocean. There are now four fish hatcheries which raise and release young salmon. When they return to the hatchery where they were born, they increase the size of the summer runs. About one-third of the catch in a typical year is of hatchery fish.

This combination of 'wild' and 'hatchery' salmon increases the ecosystem capacity. The fish breeding business is called aquaculture.

The biggest problem we face in managing the Sound's fish stocks comes once the salmon swim beyond US national waters. Out in the Pacific they can be swept up by the huge trawl nets of the Japanese factory ships. Then we never get to catch them!

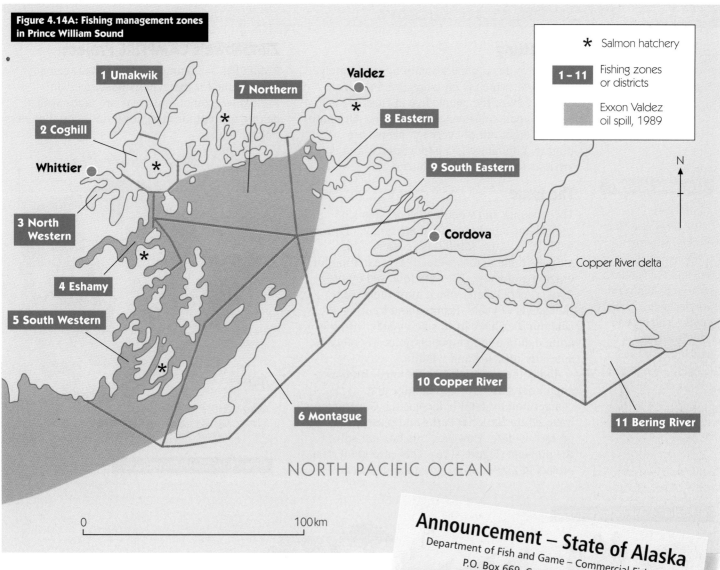

Figure 4.14A: Fishing management zones in Prince William Sound

* Salmon hatchery

1 – 11 Fishing zones or districts

Exxon Valdez oil spill, 1989

1 Umakwik
2 Coghill
7 Northern
Valdez
8 Eastern
9 South Eastern
Whittier
Cordova
3 North Western
Copper River delta
4 Eshamy
5 South Western
10 Copper River
11 Bering River
6 Montague

NORTH PACIFIC OCEAN

0   100km

N

Questions

8 Study Figure 4.10.
  a Describe the life cycle of salmon.
  b Why does Marilyn Nielsen need to count the numbers of salmon returning?

9 Study Figures 4.11 and 4.14.
  a What does Stefan Marking mean by the 'escapement run'?
  b How does the ADFG policy work to conserve salmon stocks in Prince William Sound?

10 Study Figure 4.12. Name three factors which affect how Joseph and Sunny make their living.

11 Study Figure 4.13. Use David Stephenson's account to explain how resource managers can increase the productive capacity of an ecosystem.➧

12 Use the example of the Prince William Sound salmon fishing industry to show what is meant by sustainable resource management and the problems associated with it.➧

Announcement – State of Alaska
Department of Fish and Game – Commercial Fisheries
P.O. Box 669, Cordova, Alaska 99574

PRINCE WILLIAM SOUND SALMON ANNOUNCEMENT

4.00 p.m. Tuesday, August 13, 1991

Pink Salmon Returns The harvest from the 12-hour commercial fishing period on Monday August 12, is approximately 3,500,000 salmon. The cumulative harvest of PWSAC hatchery and wild stock pinks is approximately 6.8 million fish.
The next commercial fishery will occur on Wednesday, August 14. This fishing period will be 12 hours in duration. This period will be a clock opening and will commence at 8.00 a.m. and close at 8.00 p.m. Waters open to commercial salmon fishing will be:
1) All waters of the Esther Subdistrict.
2) All waters of the Unakwik Inlet (Northern District).
3) All waters of the port San Juan Subdistrict and Elrington Subdistrict.
Fishermen are reminded that there is limited processing capacity available for Wednesday's opener and not all processing companies will be represented on the grounds.

Figure 4.14B: Declaring an 'opener'

Main activity

Report writing.

Do you know?

? Zimbabwe experiences seasonal rainfall patterns.

? The main species of animals which attract tourists to Zimbabwe are elephants, lions, giraffes and baboons.

? 'Subsistence agriculture' means growing enough crops to feed the family with only a small amount to trade.

The setting

Zimbabwe has a population of approximately 11 million, which is growing at 2.5% a year. Almost 70% of the people live in rural areas and depend upon subsistence agriculture. Although at least eight out of every ten people are literate, Zimbabwe is a poor country, and is anxious to develop its resources.

The issue

The savanna and woodland ecosystems of central and southern Africa are famous for their wildlife. Because rainfall is seasonal, the animals roam across wide areas, searching for grazing and water. They are followed by the lions, cheetahs, etc. which hunt them. For thousands of years, farming and hunting communities have lived side-by-side with the animal, bird and fish populations. There was space for humans and wildlife.

Today the situation has changed. Human populations are growing rapidly, and competition for land is increasing. Governments have set up National Parks and reserves to protect wildlife. However, this has not solved the problem (Figure 4.15). This case study of a project in Zimbabwe suggests an answer.

Zimbabwe's CAMPFIRE Project

CAMPFIRE = Communal Areas Management Programme for Indigenous Resources. In Zimbabwe, communal areas are lands which belong to communities, not to individual owners (Figure 4.16).

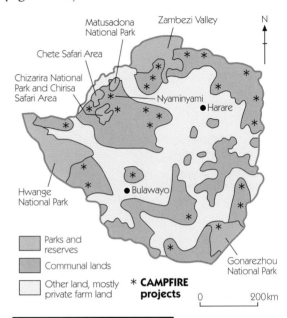

Parks and reserves
Communal lands
Other land, mostly private farm land
* CAMPFIRE projects

Figure 4.16: CAMPFIRE projects

A Without conservation policies

- Populations grow
- More food is needed
- More land is cleared, settled and farmed

- Natural habitats are lost
- Less land for wildlife
- Animals are hunted
- Species are reduced

B With parks and reserves

- Population still growing and pressing against park boundaries
- Land is overused because of lack of space
- Wild animals such as elephants raid farmland

- Parks protect wildlife and habitats
- Hunting is banned
- Animal numbers increase and wander outside parks to search for food

Figure 4.15: People and wildlife compete for resources

A government official explains the idea: 'Until now, people have seen animals only as a threat to their lives, property and crops. But once they realise the economic advantages of preserving wildlife, they quickly come to like the idea of using it rather than destroying it.'

Wildlife does bring in money. Tourists come from all over the world to look at, photograph and, where it is permitted, to hunt Africa's fabulous wildlife. Too often, however, local communities get few benefits from conserving the wildlife for tourists. Governments and tour companies organise the tourism and take most of the profits.

The CAMPFIRE approach is different. It is the local people who control and manage the tourism. Starting in 1988, the Zimbabwe government has encouraged groups of communities to set up district CAMPFIRE committees and trusts to make decisions (Figures 4.17 and 4.18). By 1995, there were 24 projects.

Example A: The Nyaminyami District
Simon Moyo, a village elder:

Our communal lands lie on the shores of Lake Kariba. We have 35,000 people but in ten years there will be twice as many. This is a dry region and our crops sometimes fail. Wild animals damage our crops and can be dangerous. But we know they are attractive to tourists. Our district has 500 elephants, 4500 buffalo and 15,000 impala (antelope.).

We've had tourists for a long time because we're near a National Park. But most of the money went to the government and the tour companies. So, we were keen to join CAMPFIRE. Our project is run by a Community Trust. This is really a committee made up of three groups: the local community, the National Park Department and the tour companies.

The National Park people advise us on how to guide safari tourists and how many hunting permits we should allow. This is our 'quota' – how many animals may be killed without affecting the resource. The tour companies pay us a fee for every hunting permit. In our first year, 1989, these fees were US $250,000. This has slowly increased.

Figure 4.17

Example B: The Hurungwe District
Cherry Bird, a Community Development worker:

In my district, the project has been based on a hunting contract with a safari company. In our first year, 1992, this brought in US $140,000. Over 80% of this went back into the local communities. The rest was spent in running our District Council.

Every year, the big issue is: 'Cash or projects?' In dry years, like 1992, when crops fail, most communities take the cash to share out to families. In good years, like 1994, communities tend to use much of the money for local projects. So far, we've bought grinding mills for grain and beehives for honey. We've built schools, health clinics, community halls, and are starting on simple tourist accommodation.

There have been some problems. There are always arguments about how the money should be spent. Also, the men make most of the decisions and control the projects. Yet women do most of the hard work! Local people still need to improve their skills in managing wildlife and looking after tourists. Also, they need help in running the new equipment and farm projects started up with CAMPFIRE cash.

Local leaders
Decide on use of communal lands

National park staff
Give advice on wildlife management and how many animals may be hunted

Tour companies
Negotiate contracts for photo and hunting safarais and pass on fees to the local trust

Each community decides how to use its share

Local leaders
Decide on allocation of money to communities

Money from tourism

Figure 4.18: A CAMPFIRE committee at work

▼ Question

Use the materials to write a report, not more than 250 words long, on the CAMPFIRE Project for your local newspaper. Use journalistic style and format, e.g. headline, personal quotes, map, cartoon. If you have access to a suitable software package, then you may wish to design your article as part of a newspaper page.➡

Review

● Sustainable resource use must work within the productive capacity of a resource.
● The fish resources of Prince William Sound, Alaska, are managed sustainably by controlling where and when boats can fish.
● Hatcheries are one way of increasing the productive capacity of a fish resource.
● Resource conservation and development can work together if local communities are involved.
● The CAMPFIRE Project, Zimbabwe, is a community-based scheme where local people benefit from wildlife conservation and nature-based tourism.

5 Energy impacts

CASE STUDY: Oman

Key ideas

● Demand for oil grows as world energy use increases.
● A small number of countries have become rich by developing their oil reserves.
● Oil is a non-renewable resource.

Main activity

The use of information to assess the sustainability of development.

Do you know?

? A renewable resource is one that replaces itself, such as water or wind.
? A non-renewable energy resource does not replace itself after use, e.g. coal, oil.
? The main users of oil in the world are the USA and Western Europe. The main suppliers are the USA and the Middle East.

Energy demand is growing

We often hear about the need to conserve energy. Cars are advertised as being 'fuel efficient'; buildings are designed to reduce the loss of heat. Yet the world used 20% more energy in 1994 than in 1980. This is because there are more people, and because for the majority, standards of living are improving.

Oil is the main source of energy used to satisfy this growing demand. As a result, discovering oil is rather like winning the National Lottery – one day you are poor; the next day you are rich! For example, think of the countries around the Persian Gulf (Figure 5.1). Forty years ago they were mostly poor desert countries. Today some are among the richest in the world. All because they are sitting on at least 50% of the world's oil reserves.

FACTFILE: Oman

Area	212,000 square kilometres (about the size of the British Isles)
Climate and environment	Hot desert, rugged mountains, sand dunes and plains, salt marshes
Population	2.1 million (1995)
Annual growth rate	4.5%
Religion	Muslim

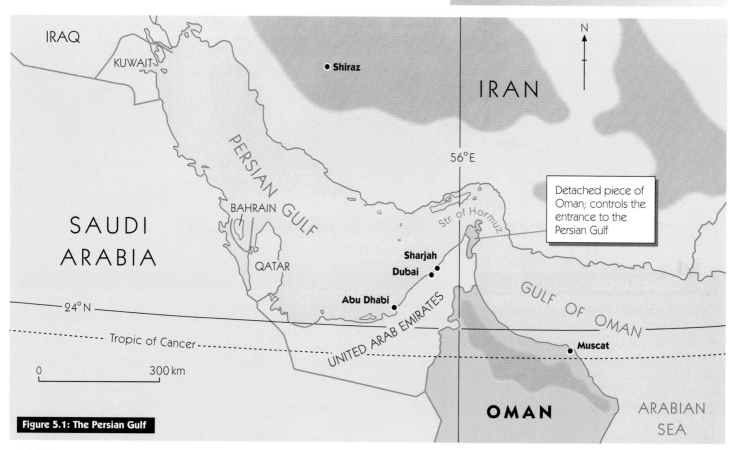

Figure 5.1: The Persian Gulf

As lottery winners have found out, however, sudden wealth may bring problems as well as benefits. So, wealth from oil can be a mixed blessing (Figure 5.2). Oman is one of the Persian Gulf countries which has become rich from oil, and in this case study we shall try to answer these important questions:

● How has the wealth been used, and who has benefited?

● What will happen when the oil reserves run out?

Figure 5.3: Nomads of the desert

Oman's oil revolution

When the first oil was pumped in 1967, Oman was still a poor, traditional country. Only 7% of the people lived in towns along the coast. The rest were mainly nomads who moved with their camels, goats and sheep to find grazing (Figure 5.3). There were only ten kilometres of tarmac roads; only one-quarter of children went to school; only one in ten families had a safe water supply; there were few doctors or hospitals. By 1997, so much had changed:

● Oman earns US $3 billion a year from oil and natural gas.

● A pipeline network pumps oil and gas to huge new refineries and ports, for loading into tankers.

● Over 800,000 barrels of oil a day are exported.

● More than 15% of the population live in the rapidly growing towns and cities.

● Urban settlements have electricity, water supply, sewage and phone systems; many buildings have air conditioning.

● Less than one-half of the population depend upon agriculture (Figure 5.4).

● Almost 90% of children go to school.

● Two-thirds of families have a safe water supply.

● Oman has 6000 kilometres of tarmac road and an international airport.

The good	The bad	The ugly
Can bring great wealth very quickly. This allows rapid investment and change.	It is a non-renewable resource and may be quickly used up. What happens then?	Can bring pollution and changes to the environment.

Figure 5.2: Oil – a mixed blessing

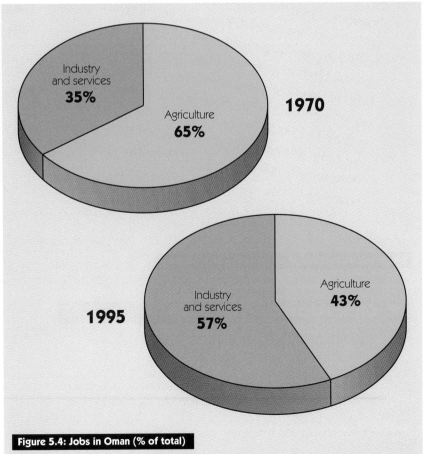

Figure 5.4: Jobs in Oman (% of total)

Many visitors to Oman notice the old and the new side by side. Peter Range is a journalist who made his first visit in 1994, only 25 years after the oil revolution took off. The extracts from his diary in Figure 5.5 record some of the impacts of the changes.

Monday: I've come during winter – only 80°F during the day. As I speed along the expressway from the airport to Muscat, the capital, I have the feeling I'm in a miniature Los Angeles: white houses everywhere; palm trees lining the roads.

Tuesday: I'm visiting the home of a businessman. As we drive here in his sleek Mercedes, he spends the time talking business on his mobile phone. When we first arrive he pushes remote control buttons to adjust twin satellite dishes on the roof. He then watches CNN and BBC television. But when we eat, he sits on the floor and eats rice and meat with his fingers, like any Bedouin in the desert. His wife and daughters keep on their veils because I am a visitor.

Wednesday: Today I've driven 300 miles [480 kilometres] into the desert to a Bedouin camp. We eat on a carpet under the stars and will sleep in a traditional tent. All around us, four-wheel drives and pickups are parked. Kanadish, my host, still herds his camels and goats. His family moves several times a year to find grazing. Two of his brothers and both sons have jobs with the government and in the oilfields and so come and go in their trucks. Government lorries deliver water to the camp. His granddaughters are driven to a state school each day, but the boys stay in a state boarding school.

Friday: This is Sidab, a fishing village near Muscat. I'm going fishing with Talib. He still catches the fish with lines and hooks in the old-fashioned way. But his old wooden boat is gone. He has a new fibreglass boat, powered by big Japanese outboard engines. The government gave him one-half of the money to pay for it.

Sunday: I'm being shown round the modern Royal Hospital, finished in 1987. This is a high-tech hospital. It has over 600 beds and does all kinds of advanced surgery. Most of the doctors, as in the rest of Oman, are foreigners. But there is a new University Medical School and the aim is to replace them.

Monday: As I fly home, I'm thinking back on my trip. One thing strikes me – I seem to have spent most of my time talking with men. Oman is rich and is modernising quickly, but is still very much a traditional Muslim country. Most women wear traditional clothes, don't mix freely outside the family, and do not have jobs. I was told that only 15% of the labour force are women.

Figure 5.5: Impressions of Oman – Peter Range's diary

▼ Questions

Read Peter Range's diary carefully (Figure 5.5).

1 Make two lists of the things he records:
   ● Aspects of traditional life which survive.
   ● Evidence of changes caused by wealth from oil development.
2 Name three ways in which the government has used money from oil.
3 Give three ways in which people's lives have changed.

Plenty of jobs – but who gets them?

A government official has said: 'We export oil and import people'. What did he mean?

Many developing countries have problems finding enough people with useful skills. This occurs especially when development is rapid, as with oil development. One answer is to import workers. This has happened in Oman, and in 1995 there were 400,000 foreign workers. They made up one-half of the labour force, and fell into two main groups (Figure 5.6).

The future for Oman

Oman is facing some hard facts:
● Oil is a non-renewable resource.
● At present, oil brings in 95% of Oman's export earnings.
● Estimates say that the oil reserves will run out by the year 2015.
● Once construction is over, the oil industry is not labour-intensive, i.e. does not employ large numbers of people.
● Population is growing at more than 4% a year. Over one-half of Omanis are younger than 15 years, and will be needing jobs.
● Oman is a desert country, and water resources are already fully used.

The Oman government is aware of the problems. Sayyid Haithan, a government minister, said in 1995: 'We are trying to prepare for the next phase. People will survive, but not at the same level of luxury as today.' He suggests several possible answers:
● We have to make more jobs for Omanis. The government is insisting that industries and businesses give increasing proportions of jobs to our people.
● We have to diversify our economy. This means encouraging new industries, especially manufacturing, which will carry on when the oil is gone. The government gives grants and loans to foreign and local companies to start up on modern industrial estates.
● We could develop tourism. Oman has beautiful beaches, constant sunshine and grand scenery. We are against mass package tourism

Professionals
Skilled professionals, e.g. engineers, doctors, teachers, lawyers, managers. For example, in 1995 there were at least 2000 foreign doctors in Oman. One of the aims of the new schools and universities is to train Omanis to take over these jobs.

Workers
Workers and labourers for the oil, construction and service industries. At first there were simply not enough local people. Today, as Omanis become educated, they want high wages to work as professionals and for the government as civil servants. Workers brought in from India, Pakistan, Bangladesh, Sri Lanka and the Philippines will work for lower wages.

Figure 5.6: Foreign workers in Oman

because of the impacts on our Omani culture.
● We must control our population growth. The government has family planning schemes to reduce family size. Also, we shall allow fewer foreign workers into the country.
● There has to be more efficient use of water, and perhaps **desalination** plants to purify seawater.

▼ Questions

4 Give two reasons why Oman has brought in so many foreign workers.
5 Is Oman likely to depend so much on foreign labour in the future? What type of worker will the country continue to need?
6 Use the example of Oman to show the problems faced by a LEDC (Less Economically Developed Country) in making its development sustainable. ➡

Review

● World demand for oil is growing.
● Oman has based its development upon its oil resources.
● Oil is a non-renewable resource, so if Oman's development is to be sustainable, its economy must be diversified.
● Oman is trying to balance modernisation with the preservation of its traditional culture.

Key ideas

● Wildlife and humans often compete for the same space and resources.
● Some forms of economic development may conflict with the way ecosystems work.
● People hold very contrasting opinions about how resources should be used.

Do you know?

❓ An ecosystem is made up of a set of components which depend upon each other.
❓ Each living species has a place or niche in an ecosystem and depends upon the whole ecosystem as the habitat in which it can survive.
❓ The type of geological conditions where oil and gas reserves are found.
❓ The location and supply of oil and gas in the world.
❓ The nature of permafrost and what happens when structures are built on it.

Main activity

Decision making, letter writing.

Putting wildlife first

An increasing number of countries are setting up special areas to protect wildlife and the environments in which they live. This is happening because:
● Humans are using more and more of the world's resources.
● As natural ecosystems and wildlife become threatened, people realise how precious they are, and try to conserve them (Figure 5.7).

These protected areas are given different names, such as parks, reserves or refuges. However, their common purpose is to conserve the habitat and the species which depend upon that habitat.

In the USA the government have set up a system of National Wildlife Refuges. There are over 500 of them, totalling almost 38 million hectares. There is at least one in every one of the 50 states (see Case Study: Bosque del Apache, New Mexico, page 24). Wildlife protection is their primary purpose. However, many contain valuable resources such as timber or minerals. This puts the refuges under great pressure from powerful corporations who want to develop the resources. Tourists and hunters are attracted too.

More than 50% of the total area covered by National Wildlife Refuges is in Alaska (Figure 5.9). The largest is the Arctic National Wildlife Refuge (ANWR). It takes in part of Alaska's

Figure 5.7: 'Koalas will only survive if the eucalyptus woodland on which they depend, survives.' (Wilson's Promontory National Park, Australia)

North Slope, where some of the richest oil and gas reserves are found. This case study sets out the issue – conservation or development, which shall it be?

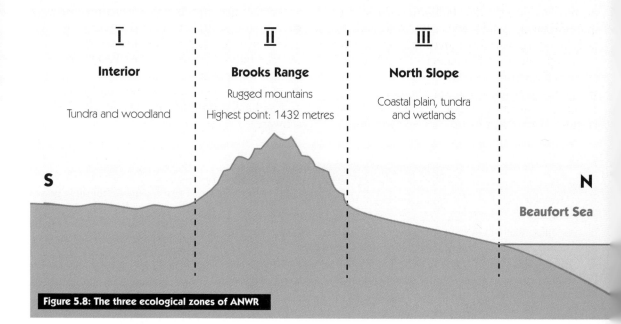

I	II	III
Interior	**Brooks Range**	**North Slope**
	Rugged mountains	Coastal plain, tundra and wetlands
Tundra and woodland	Highest point: 1432 metres	

S

N

Beaufort Sea

Figure 5.8: The three ecological zones of ANWR

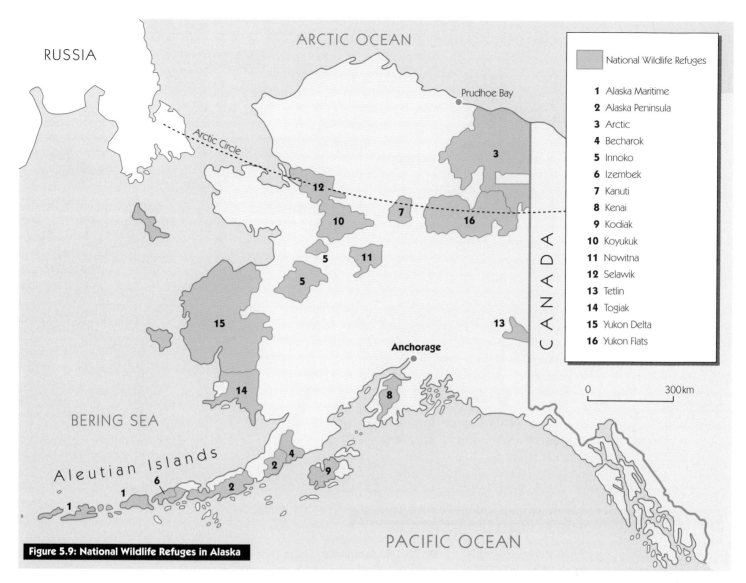

Figure 5.9: National Wildlife Refuges in Alaska

Key: National Wildlife Refuges

1 Alaska Maritime
2 Alaska Peninsula
3 Arctic
4 Becharok
5 Innoko
6 Izembek
7 Kanuti
8 Kenai
9 Kodiak
10 Koyukuk
11 Nowitna
12 Selawik
13 Tetlin
14 Togiak
15 Yukon Delta
16 Yukon Flats

Figure 5.10: Caribou in the Alaskan tundra

ANWR – The case for conservation

● ANWR spreads across almost 8 million hectares and contains three main ecological zones (Figure 5.8). The conflict is centred on zone III – the low tundra and wetlands of the North Slope.

● The refuge protects many species of wildlife. However, ANWR's main purpose is to conserve space and habitat for the largest caribou herds remaining in North America (Figure 5.10).

● Most caribou are migratory animals. Up to 400,000 caribou spend the harsh winters scattered across the woods and tundra south of the Brooks Range (zone I on Figure 5.8). As temperatures rise in the spring, they move north to the coastal plain.

● The largest herd is known as the Porcupine Herd with about 170,000 animals. You can follow the rhythm of their year on Figure 5.11. The map shows that during the winter they are dispersed across a vast area. In the spring they gradually form three main groups and move slowly northwards.

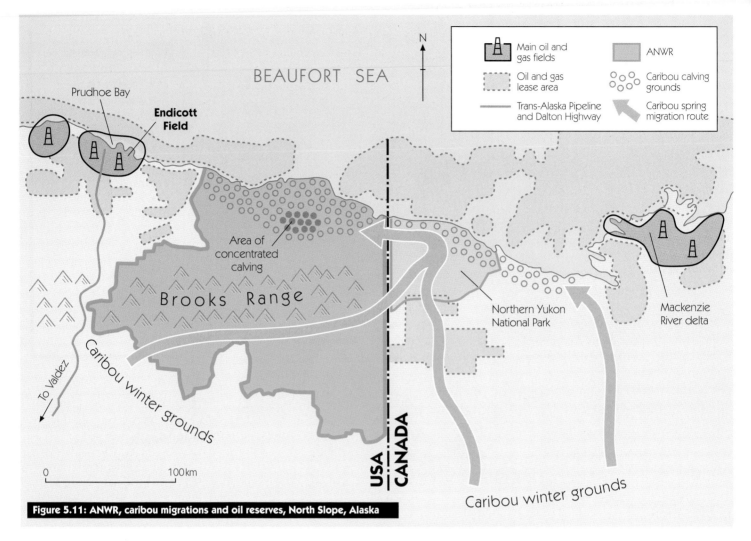

Figure 5.11: ANWR, caribou migrations and oil reserves, North Slope, Alaska

Legend:
- Main oil and gas fields
- Oil and gas lease area
- Trans-Alaska Pipeline and Dalton Highway
- ANWR
- Caribou calving grounds
- Caribou spring migration route

BEAUFORT SEA

Prudhoe Bay

Endicott Field

Area of concentrated calving

Brooks Range

Caribou winter grounds

To Valdez

USA | CANADA

Northern Yukon National Park

Mackenzie River delta

Caribou winter grounds

0   100 km

● After a journey of up to 500 kilometres, this great herd assembles on the coastal plain to spend the summer. The calves are born and reared here. The coastal **tundra** provides good grazing. The animals use the shallow waters of the wetlands and coastal fringe to escape from the vast numbers of mosquitoes which torment them. In the autumn they drift southwards.

● ANWR and the Northern Yukon National Park in Canada are vital if their summer habitat is to be protected. There is nowhere else for the caribou to spend the summer months.

● Figure 5.11 shows that oil and gas development is pressing in upon ANWR from three sides. There are known to be reserves beneath the coastal plain between Prudhoe Bay and the Mackenzie Delta. The environmental impact of allowing development inside ANWR would be great: habitat would be lost, and female caribou would be disturbed during their calving season. There is evidence that calving is reduced in oilfield areas outside ANWR.

● ANWR only protects 180 out of 2000 kilometres along the Arctic shoreline; the oil companies are able to drill along the rest. Surely they do not need this last stretch.

● The oil companies claim that they use modern techniques which reduce the impacts and chances of pollution (Figure 5.12). However, any built structures affect the fragile **permafrost** and the record on pollution is not good (Figure 5.13).

● Even if all the oil from beneath ANWR is pumped out, it will only be about the amount that the US consumes in one year.

Figure 5.12: Oil installations, Prudhoe Bay, North Slope, Alaska

BP denies dumping toxic waste in Alaska

BP is at the centre of a wide-ranging criminal inquiry into the allegedly illegal dumping of thousands of tons of toxic waste in its oil fields in northern Alaska.

Environmental experts fear the secret dumping poses a threat to local wildlife, including polar bears, fish and seals.

The American Environmental Protection Agency (EPA) and the FBI have mounted an enquiry.

The dumping is believed to be the largest example of illegal waste disposal since oil companies started exploiting the Alaskan oil reserves in the 1970s.

Any prosecution will also undermine BP's attempts to extend its drilling operations into Alaska's Arctic Refuge, home to many protected populations of wildlife, including caribou and 300,000 snow geese. The Refuge, described as 'America's Serengeti', is the last unspoilt wilderness on the continent.

The inquiry centres on Endicott Field in the remote North Slope area of Alaska. Endicott is located in an estuary which is a rich feeding habitat for migrating fish.

The EPA was alerted after an employee working in Endicott reported routine illegal dumping of toxic waste in underground reservoirs. EPA officials and conservationists have warned that the toxins could seep into ground water and into the Beaufort Sea, posing a threat to wildlife.

The man, who worked for Doyon Drilling, a BP sub-contractor, was repeatedly instructed to put toxic waste, including paints, paint thinners, hydraulic fluid, used oil and glycol, into the underground wells. When he refused because it was illegal he was told that the law was irrelevant because 'nobody lives on the North Slope anyway'.

BP, as the company in charge of the oil fields, is responsible for its sub-contractors. 'We conducted our own thorough investigation and found no evidence of wrongdoing by BP staff,' a spokesman said.

Figure 5.13: By Tim Kelsey and David Leppard of the Sunday Times

Figure 5.14: Oil production in Alaska

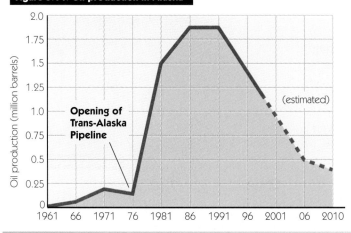

ANWR – The oil companies' case

● Americans use more oil products than anyone else in the world. At least one-half of this oil demand is imported. Is this necessary, when there are unused reserves within the USA?

● Alaska has become rich because of the oil from the North Slope. But production from the present fields is already declining seriously (Figure 5.14). The Trans-Alaska Pipeline System (TAPS) cost billions of dollars, but is no longer being used fully. Alaska needs the jobs and the money from oil and gas. The oil companies need to continue to be able to use their expensive equipment.

● There are believed to be up to 9 billion barrels of oil reserves beneath ANWR. Modern techniques allow a group of wells to be clustered much closer together than 20 years ago. This means that the gravel pads on which the well heads stand can be much smaller. There will be minimal impact on the tundra and the underlying permafrost.

● The oil companies claim that only 1% of the coastal plain within ANWR will be affected.

● The oil companies claim that caribou numbers around the oilfields have increased. The animals avoid the immediate installation areas and have plenty of space across the vast North Slope.

● There is already a law, passed in 1989, called the 'no net loss' law. This states that for every hectare of wetland taken for development, an oil company must create one hectare of wetland habitat. So, there should be the same space for caribou.

Review

● The North Slope oilfields have been Alaska's main source of income since they opened in 1976.
● The existing oilfields are declining in production.
● ANWR, and especially the coastal plain tundra within it, are vital for the large herds of migratory caribou.
● The oil companies want to develop the oil reserves beneath ANWR, but conservationists oppose it.
● The oil companies claim that impact from development will be minimal; conservationists claim that the caribou will be severely disturbed.

▼ Questions

1 Study Figure 5.14.
  a In which year did the Trans-Alaska Pipeline open?
  b The story of oil production in Alaska falls into four phases. Define (give the years of start and finish) and describe each of these phases.

2 Study Figure 5.13.
  a What is the cause of the alleged pollution?
  b What is being polluted and what are being threatened?
  c Why has the employee decided to complain?

3 Study Figures 5.8 and 5.11.
  a Describe the location, size and character of ANWR.
  b Describe briefly the location and distribution of the oilfields and oil leases. Include their location in relation to ANWR.
  c Why is ANWR so important for conservation?

4 Decision time: Write a letter to be sent to the Governor of Alaska, suggesting an answer to the issue of whether oil development should be allowed in ANWR, giving your reasons. ➔

5 Use the ANWR example to discuss the statement that there may be no one 'right' answer to some environmental conflicts. ➔

6 Assessing development

CASE STUDY: Chile: indices of development

Key ideas

● Sets of indicators are used to measure development.
● By using these indicators, countries can be grouped into three classes: LEDCs, NICs and MEDCs.

Do you know?

? Population change can be understood by studying growth rates, population structure, and birth and death rates.
? 'Quality of life' includes standard of living, health, education and security.
? Industries are divided into categories: primary, secondary, tertiary and quaternary.
? The difference between economic growth and development is that growth refers to the increasing size of the economy whereas development is the process of meeting people's needs and improving society.

Main activity

Data interpretation and decision making.

The issue

Books and atlases often show countries divided into three classes: More Economically Developed Country (MEDC); Newly Industrialised Country (NIC); Less Economically Developed Country (LEDC). When we see such lists or maps, one question we need to ask is: 'What measures have been used to describe a particular country in this way?' We are asking, 'What is meant by "development"?'

This case study introduces some of the measures commonly used. Then figures are given for one country, Chile. Your main task is to use these figures to decide whether Chile is a MEDC, a NIC, or a LEDC – or none of these!

Measuring development

Figure 6.3 is a checklist. It describes some of the popular measures or indices used to assess a country's stage of **development**. There are four categories: population, quality of life, economy and trade. As you use the list, remember four things: first, it is only a general guide and does not contain all possible measures. Second, 'high' and 'low' vary from one characteristic to another. Notice that some guidelines are given to help you. Third, for some countries all the information may not be available or up-to-date. Fourth, no one country will have *all* the characteristics described for a MEDC, or a NIC, or a LEDC.

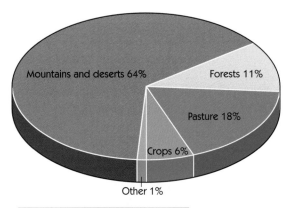

Figure 6.1: Land use in Chile, 1995

Mountains and deserts 64%
Forests 11%
Pasture 18%
Crops 6%
Other 1%

Figure 6.2: Chile – location

Chile

Chile is an unusual shape. It is a long, narrow country, stretching 4000 kilometres along the south west coast of South America (Figure 6.2). This length, and the rugged Andes Mountains, make internal communications and links with other countries difficult. Chile extends from hot deserts in the north to cool, wet forests in the south. Central Chile has a Mediterranean climate, and is the core of the country, with the capital, Santiago (1994 population 5.7 million). The country covers almost 757,000 square kilometres, but 64% is classed as 'unproductive' mountain and desert (Figure 6.1).

Characteristic			
Population	**MEDC**	**NIC**	**LEDC**
Growth	Low growth rates *Less than 1% a year*	Rapidly falling growth rates	High growth rates *Over 2% a year*
Birth rate	Low *Less than 12/1000*	Moderate and falling	High but falling *Over 30/1000*
Death rate	Low *Less than 10/1000*	Moderate and falling	High, falling faster than BR *Over 20/1000*
Length of life	Long *More than 65 years*	Averages rising rapidly	Short and improving *Less than 50 years*
Structure	'Ageing': high proportions in older age groups	'Mature': young proportions falling, older proportions rising	'Youthful': high proportions in younger age groups
Distribution	High proportions in cities, with extensive sprawl *Over 70% in cities*	A few large cities dominant, often in a core region	High proportions still rural, but a few rapidly expanding cities *Less than 30% in cities*
Quality of life			
Infant mortality	Very low rates *Less than 10/1000*	Rapidly falling to moderate rates	High rates, but falling *More than 60/1000*
Doctors and hospitals	High provision, high standards	Good provision, especially in cities	Low and variable provision and standards
Domestic water and sewage	High proportions in urban and rural areas connected to sewage systems *Over 80%*	Majority connected to water/sewage systems, especially in cities	Low proportions of families connected to water/sewage systems *Less than 40%*
Literacy	High in all regions *Over 90%*	Rising rapidly, especially in cities	Low, but rising *Less than 50%*
Higher education	High numbers *Over 20%*	Numbers rising rapidly	Low numbers *Less than 5%*
Economy			
Structure	High proportions in industry, especially service industries	Well developed manufacturing; service industries growing rapidly	Mainly farming and other primary industries
Unemployment	Low to moderate *Less than 7%*	Recently fallen to low levels	Generally high *More than 15%*
Infrastructure	Well developed transport, communications and energy systems	Rapidly improving modern systems, spreading to all regions	Poorly developed transport, communications and energy systems
Trade			
Imports	Wide range of industrial and food products	Increasing range of consumer goods	Highly dependent on industrial imports
Exports	Wide range of industrial products, capital and consumer goods	Commercial crops and an increasing range of industrial products	Narrow range of primary products and raw materials

Figure 6.3: Checklist – Some popular measures of development

▼ Questions

The following is the key question for you to answer: 'Is Chile a MEDC, or a NIC, or a LEDC, or does it have the features of more than one class?' The resources on pages 46–49 provide information from all four categories on your checklist.

1 Take the first checklist item (population growth) and read the description for each class of country.

2 Look carefully at the population growth figures for Chile (Figure 6.4).

3 Decide which class of country (MEDC; NIC; LEDC) Chile falls into in terms of population growth.

4 Repeat this exercise for each item on your checklist where there is information for Chile.

5 Draw a copy of the checklist, but leave the description boxes empty. As you make your decisions, place ticks in the correct boxes.

6 You may find an item – say unemployment – that does not fit neatly into any class. In this case, use the box spaces to describe Chile's figures and why they do not fit into any one class.

7 When you have filled in your own checklist, write a brief report stating which class of country you think Chile falls into. Give reasons for your decision. You may decide that Chile does not fit into any one class. If so, state your reasons why.

Population growth

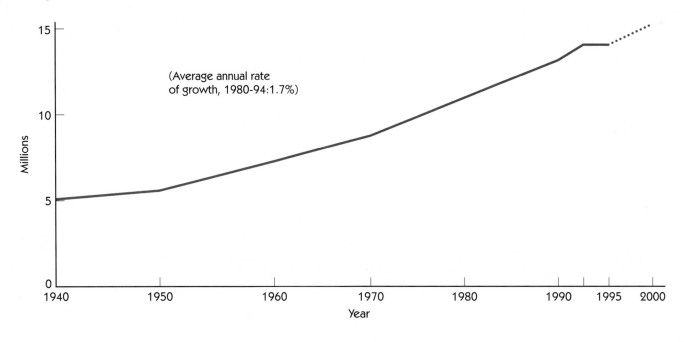

	1960	1980	1994
Birth rate (rate/1000 population)	38	24	22
Death rate (rate/1000 population)	12	7	6
Average length of life (years)	60	67	74

Figure 6.4: Population characteristics and structure

	1960	1980	1994
Infant mortality (rate/1000 live births)	40	33	13
Numbers in higher education	65,000	119,000	327,000
Literacy rate (% total population)	70	94	95

Figure 6.5: Quality of life

Employment structure (1994)

Rank	Sector	Number ('000)	% of total
1	Commerce and trade	921	18
2	Agriculture	781	15
3	Industry	821	16
4	Transport	356	6.5
5	Construction	372	7
6	Mining	92	2
	Other	1857	35.5
	Total	*5200*	*100*

In 1994, of the 5.2 million people who had jobs, 2.1 million were in Santiago, including 55% of all manufacturing industry workers. In 1980, 3.6 million were employed; in 1994 the total was 5.2 million.

Unemployment: In 1980, 20% of workers in Chile were unemployed. In 1994 this figure was 6%.

Importance of economic activity sectors, 1994

Rank	Sector	% total output value
1	Manufacturing	19
2	Commerce and trade	18
3	Financial services	14
4	Mining	9
5	Transport	8
6	Agriculture and forestry	7

Figure 6.6: Chile's economy

Imports: the top five (% of total by value)

Product	1994
Metal products and machinery	50
Chemicals and oil products	17
Grade oil and coal	7
Textiles	6
Foodstuffs and drinks	4

NB: 1980 figures for imports are not available. Import sources (1994): 24% from the USA; 9% from Japan; 9% from Brazil.

Exports: the top five (% of total by value)

Product	1980	1994
Copper	46	36
Other minerals	10	7.5
Food products	9	19
Pulp and paper products	6	8
Fruit	3	8.5

Export markets (1994): 17% to the USA; 17% to Japan; 16% to the rest of Asia.

Figure 6.7: Chile's trade

Review

● Indicators are a useful way of measuring development. However, a country may not have reached the same level of development on all indicators. So, it may not be easy to place that country in one development class.
● Chile is a good example of a country where the indicators fall into different classes.

New industrial giants

Key ideas

● Factors influencing industrial location change over time.
● One of the main aims of a company is to keep production costs down.
● **Globalisation** is one of the most important features of modern industry.
● The industries of a country must adapt to changes in technology and demand.

Do you know?

? The names of the four main islands which make up Japan.
? The main cities and population of Japan.
? The factors which influence industrial location.
? What we mean by primary, secondary, tertiary and quaternary industries.
? The main factors which influence how much a product or a service costs.

Main activity

Use of information to assess industrial structure and location.

The shrinking planet

Think about these examples:
● Open an account with the Midland Bank and you will be dealing with the Hong Kong and Shanghai Bank, who own Midland.
● Buy a Vauxhall car and you will be helping the profits of General Motors, an American company.
● This book is published by Stanley Thornes (Publishers) Ltd of Cheltenham, which is owned by a Dutch corporation.

These are three examples of what is called 'globalisation'. Economic activity is increasingly controlled by huge **multinational** or **transnational corporations**. They make their products in many different countries. We can buy the same products in countries all over the world (Figure 7.1).

Communication systems can move information, ideas and money around the world

Figure 7.1: This is a Japanese Mazda car in Arizona, USA. The same model can be bought in Britain and many other countries.

in an instant. Companies move their offices and factories to where demand is growing, and where costs of production are lowest (Figure 7.2). Many industries today are more 'footloose' than in the past. That is, they can move more easily and are less closely tied to a particular location.

The two case studies in this unit show how globalisation works. First, the 'economic miracle' of Japan has been built on making and selling products all over the world. Second, the success of the Nike corporation is based on making their footwear and clothing wherever labour costs are cheapest.

50,000 JOBS IN TEXTILES COULD GO OVERSEAS

By Martyn Halsall

Fifty-thousand jobs could be lost in the textile and footwear industry by the end of the decade as manufacturers accelerate the transfer of production to the developing world.

(*The Guardian,* 13.9.96)

METRO TO GO IN SHAKE-UP AT ROVER

By Andrew Lorenz

BMW is planning to stop output of the Rover 100 – better known as the Metro – and streamline the sprawling Longbridge car plant in Birmingham.

About 8,000 of the Longbridge workforce are involved in engine manufacture. A key factor in safeguarding jobs will be whether Rover succeeds in building a new engine factory in the West Midlands. Rover wants government aid to build the plant, expected to cost about £300m initially, which would produce the next generation of small engines for both Rover and BMW. But the plan faces competition from BMW's existing engine plants in Germany and Austria.

(*The Sunday Times,* 18.8.96)

Figure 7.2: Industry on the move

An industrial revolution

At the end of the Second World War in 1945, much of Japan's industry was in ruins. By 1995, Japan had become the world's second most powerful industrial nation, after the USA (Figure 7.3). Six of the world's top 30 corporations are Japanese (Figure 7.4). Their products affect all aspects of our lives (Figure 7.5).

How did it happen?

The timeline in Figure 7.7 shows five main phases. Notice how they build up the economy: Japan started with a firm foundation of manufacturing, then broadened the range of industries and products. This involves investment in new techniques, research and forecasting which new products would become popular (Figure 7.6).

Figure 7.3: Many Japanese companies are located in new, ultra-modern complexes

World ranking	Name	Sales (US$ billion)	People employed ('000s)
[1]	General Motors (USA)	150	750)
5	Toyota	80	110
10	Hitachi	65	335
12	Matsushita Electrical Ind	60	255
16	Nissan	55	150
25	Toshiba	40	175
30	Honda	35	93

Figure 7.4: Some of the world's largest corporations (1995) – all are Japanese, except General Motors

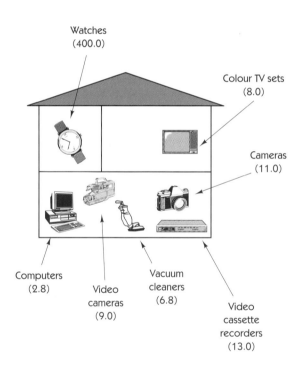

Watches (400.0)

Colour TV sets (8.0)

Cameras (11.0)

Computers (2.8)

Video cameras (9.0)

Vacuum cleaners (6.8)

Video cassette recorders (13.0)

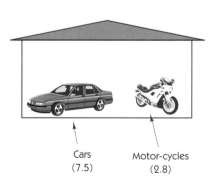

Cars (7.5)

Motor-cycles (2.8)

Figure 7.5: Output of well-known Japanese products in millions (1996)

In the 1960s we saw that world demand for motor-cycles and scooters would grow. So we looked at how the British, Italians and Americans made them. Then we built new factories, with new machinery, used fresh designs, and kept costs down. This is how we captured the mass market for bikes and scooters.

We invented the 'just-in-time' (JIT) method of manufacture. Take the car industry as an example. Parts are only ordered when we know we need them. Then they are delivered to the assembly line on the day they are needed. In the past, car makers used the 'just-in-case' (JIC) approach. They ordered large stocks of parts and stored them until they were needed. This was expensive and wasteful. Today, we have no stocks, little wastage, and lower costs.

Figure 7.6: Managers give two examples of industrial forecasting

The five phases

1 **Growth for recovery**
The government has two main policies: first, to rebuild the road, rail and port system; second, to help companies reconstruct the basic industries of steel, textiles and power generation.

2 **Growth through modernisation**
Large steel, machinery and textile companies invest in the most modern factories, shipyards and equipment. Modern factories + hard work + good organisation = low cost production and growth of exports, e.g. textiles, steel, ships.

3 **Growth through diversification**
The heavy industries provide a base for a wider range of products, e.g. toys, clothing, motor-cycles, cars. These are exported, and also sold in Japan, as people have more money to spend. Forecasting where demand will grow is important.

4 **Growth through technology**
Wealth from industry allows investment in research and technology. Japan leads the world in the 'electronics revolution', e.g. televisions, video cassette recorders, computers, microprocessors, cameras, etc.

5 **Growth through globalisation**
The large corporations, called **keiretsu**, open offices and factories all over the world. They do this for three main reasons:
● to keep labour costs down;
● to reduce imports of materials;
● to move production nearer to large markets.
Products include the most modern computer games and communications equipment.

Size of economy →

1945   1955   1965   1975   1985   1995

Year

Figure 7.7: Timeline of Japan's growth

▼ Question

1 Study Figure 7.7.
  a   Make a list of the products mentioned for each phase in Japan's growth.
  b   In one sentence, explain the Japanese government priorities for phase 1.
  c   How did Japan achieve such rapid growth in heavy industries such as steel manufacture and shipbuilding?
  d   One important aim of a developing country is to increase the variety of industries. This is called broadening the industrial base. Use the example of Japan to describe how this happens. ➡

Is Japan's industrial structure changing?

Japan today has a wide range of industries, employing 54 million people (Figure 7.8). It has the world's largest electronics industry and still leads in steel production. Yet important changes are taking place (Figures 7.9 and 7.10).

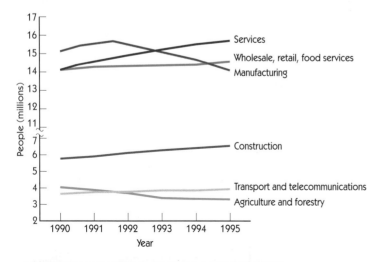

Figure 7.8: Employment in major industries, 1990–95

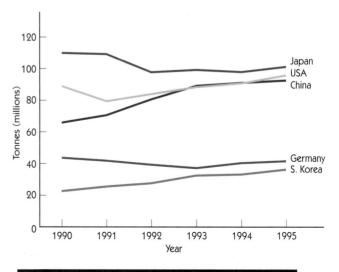

Figure 7.9: World steel production – the top five countries

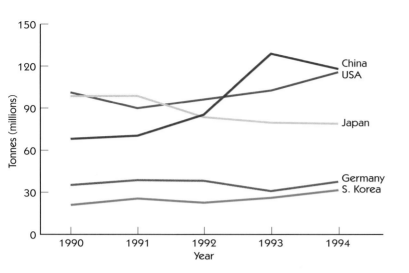

Figure 7.10: World steel consumption – the top five users

Look again at phase 5 of the timeline in Figure 7.7. One result of globalisation is that Japanese companies are making more of their products outside Japan. Here are two examples:

● By 1996, Honda was making 900,000 vehicles in the USA, Britain and South East Asia.

● In 1995 the Japanese bought 40 million Japanese-make television sets. At least 80% of them were assembled outside Japan.

This has been called the '**hollowing out**' of an economy. Headquarters, where decisions, research and finance are based, remain in Japan; manufacture is located in other countries. This process tends to develop in two stages (Figure 7.11). For example, Honda, Toyota, Sony and Toshiba all have '**transplant**' factories in Britain. Mazda has contracts with businesses spread across East and South East Asia (Figure 7.12). Remember, the 'hollowing out' process has also happened in Britain and the USA; US companies now produce 25% of their output in other countries.

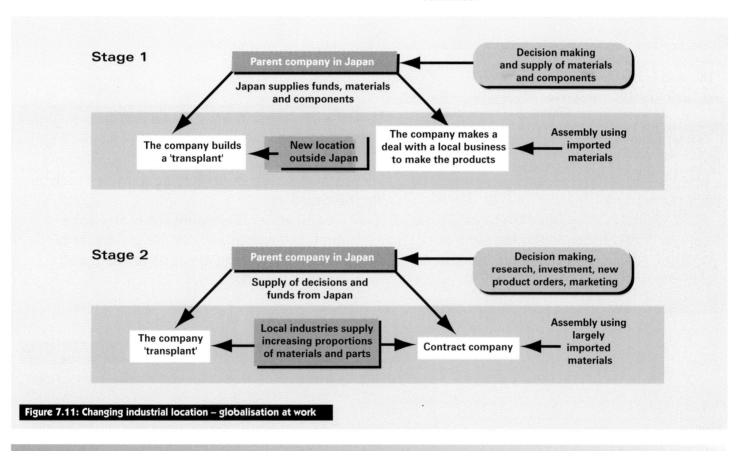

Figure 7.11: Changing industrial location – globalisation at work

▼ Questions

2 Use Figure 7.8.
   a Construct a table which shows (i) the numbers employed in the major industries and (ii) the rank order of these industries in 1990 and 1995.
   b Describe briefly the most important changes which have taken place since 1990.

3 Use Figure 7.9. In what way is the trend in steel production for Japan different from the other leading countries?

4 Study Figure 7.10.
   a How much crude steel did Japan use in (i) 1990; (ii) 1994?
   b Describe briefly the trends and changes among the world's leading users of steel between 1990 and 1995.
   c How does the graph for steel use help to explain the trend in Japan's steel output shown in Figure 7.9?

Country	Year of start-up	Assembly company	Production (vehicles)
Malaysia	1968 1989	Associated Motor Ind Cycle & Carriage Co } Bingtang Behard	2000
Indonesia	1971	P T Ismac	1500
Philippines	1974	Francisco Motors Co	2500
	1993	Columbian Autocar Co	2500
Thailand	1975	Sukosol & Mazda Motors	2500
Pakistan	1976	Sing Engineering Ltd	3000
India	1985	Swaraj Mazda Ltd	2300
Taiwan	1987	Ford Lio Ho Motor Co	4000
Vietnam	1992	Vietnam Motors Co	300
China	1992 1994	Hainan Mazda Motor Co Fuzhou Solid Motors Co	1000 5000

(NB A number of these companies now manufacture parts as well as assembling vehicles.
For example, the Thailand company now makes vehicle transmissions.)

Figure 7.12: Mazda's transplants and contracts in Asia (1995)

We can say therefore that Japan is changing from a production-based industrial structure to a knowledge-based structure.

This shift brings gains and losses:

Gains

● Lower wages and production costs, e.g. cheap electronic products.
● Production is closer to growing markets, e.g. inside China.
● Production is inside **trade barriers**, e.g. car factories in Britain are within the European Union (EU) and so avoid import restrictions.

Losses

● Workers in Japan lose their jobs (Figure 7.13).
● Workers may be plentiful and cheap, but not very skilled, e.g. in developing countries such as Indonesia.
● The Japanese corporations may lose some control over output and costs, e.g. because of financial problems in Malaysia or change of policies in the EU.

Year	%
1990	2.1
1991	2.1
1992	2.1
1993	2.6
1994	2.9
1995	3.2
1996	3.5

Figure 7.13: Unemployment in Japan (% of total workforce)

▼ Questions

5 Define what is meant by the 'hollowing out' of an economy, and use Figure 7.11 to explain how it happens.
6 Use the information in Figure 7.12. On an outline map of Eastern Asia:
  a Name Japan and mark Mazda's headquarters in southern Honshu with an *.
  b Locate and name each of the countries where Mazda cars are assembled and give the numbers produced.
  c Draw arrows joining Mazda's headquarters to the countries of production.
  d Name your map: 'Mazda: an example of "hollowing out"'.
7 As Japan's industry becomes more 'knowledge-based', suggest three types of job which will grow in numbers.
8 From Figure 7.13, describe Japan's unemployment trend since 1990 and suggest reasons for this trend.

The facts

Nike is a truly global company, using sports stars to promote its famous logo world-wide. It is an American company. In 1995, over 60 million pairs of Nike athletic footwear were sold in the USA. None of them were made in the USA.

The story

1964-70: A small company in Oregon, USA, called Blue Ribbon Sports (BRS), is a distributor for a make of Japanese athletic shoes.

1971: BRS changes its name to Nike and designs its own athletic footwear. Nike has a contract with another Japanese company to make the shoes.

1974: Nike products become more popular, but costs are rising in Japan. So, the Japanese manufacturers begin to subcontract shoe assembly to low cost factories in Taiwan and South Korea. Materials and pieces for the shoes still come from Japan.

1975–86: The Nike market goes global. The company opens factories in the USA, Hong Kong, Britain and Eire (Republic of Ireland). However, costs are too high and they are closed.

1983: Nike ends the manufacturing contracts with Japan because of high wages. Taiwan and South Korea become the production centres.

1985–95: As Taiwan and South Korea become more industrialised, they supply more of the materials and pieces as well as assembling the shoes. But costs rise here too. So, they continue to make specialist shoes, but the Taiwanese and South Korean companies subcontract low cost producers in Indonesia, Thailand, Malaysia, Vietnam and China to make mass market footwear. The bigger subcontractors can make up to 30,000 pairs a day.

The future: Competition from Adidas and other multinationals is growing. Nike now produces a full range of athletic and leisure clothing. Wearing Nike is a 'fashion statement' (Figure 7.14). The company promotes its products by expensive advertising including contracts with sports organisations, for example football associations in Europe, the US National Football League, whose players all wear the Nike logo.

Figure 7.14: For young people, the new uniform – Nike

The future

Nike will continue to seek out locations with low labour costs, and seems likely to widen its product range.

The issues

Companies such as Nike are in a huge but highly competitive market. They continually search for ways to keep costs down. So, in order to win contracts from Nike and others, businesses must offer low prices. There is growing evidence that this has caused exploitation of workers and the use of child labour (Figure 7.15).

NIKE TO TAKE A HIT IN LABOR REPORT

Nike has suspended a manager of its Vietnam plant in the wake of a report by a US-based labor group charging worker abuse in the athletic shoemaker's factories.

Thuyen Nguyen of Vietnam Labor Watch inspected Nike factories in Vietnam in both escorted and surprise visits.

He found violations of minimum wage and overtime laws, as well as physical mistreatment of workers, most of whom are women between the ages of 15 and 28.

'While Nike claims it is trying to monitor and enforce its code of conduct, its current approach to monitoring and enforcement is simply not working,' Nguyen says.

From Nguyen's report:
- As punishment for wearing non-regulation shoes, 56 women were forced to run laps around the factory. Twelve women fainted and had to be taken to a hospital.
- Inspecting pay stubs Nguyen says he saw a pattern of paying new workers subminimum wages.

Nike spokeswoman McLain Ramsey confirms Nguyen's visit to the Ho Chi Minh City plant and says company officials are 'as distressed as he is' about his report.

The manager accused of making women run laps has been suspended, she says.

The Sam Yang plant in Vietnam is owned by a Taiwanese company which Nike subcontracts, she says.

Nike has drawn fire from worker rights groups for failing to hold its subcontracted factories in Southeast Asia and China to fair labor standards. About 75% of Nike's production is done in Indonesia, China and Vietnam.

Figure 7.15: The issue of working conditions

REEBOK LEADS CHILD LABOUR PURGE

By Roger Lowe

Reebok yesterday called on its rival Nike, the market leader in trainers, to join it in a bid to end child labour and improve working conditions at their Asian factories.

Paul Fireman, the chairman and chief executive, has written to his opposite number at Nike, Phil Knight, proposing joint monitoring of factory conditions.

Reebok and Nike – who together sell 60 per cent of branded trainers – have come under pressure in Britain and America in campaigns against child labour and exploitation of Asian workers.

Reebok has taken a public stand on social issues, launching the Reebok Human Rights Award in 1988 and adopting a Human Rights Production Standard in 1992. Earlier this year, after accusations of child labour in Pakistani factories, it announced a new factory which would be monitored to ensure no children were employed.

Most trainers are made in Indonesia, the Philippines, China and other Asian countries, although production has moved from Taiwan and South Korea to lower-cost countries where trade unions are often banned.

Christian Aid says only £1.20 from the price of a £50 pair typically goes to workers who made the shoes, although huge sums are spent on marketing. It also notes that Chinese workers would have to work nine hours a day, six days a week for 15 centuries to earn the £929,113 paid to Nike boss Phil Knight last year.

The charity, in conjunction with the Fairtrade Foundation, has developed a code of conduct setting out minimum conditions and the need for independent monitoring.

But charities have also warned that a ban on child labour could be counter-productive. Oxfam argues that in very poor countries every family member has to work if they are to survive. It cites examples of Bangladeshi children forced into prostitution when factory owners stopped employing them after fears of a boycott in 1993.

▼ Questions

Study the newspaper reports in Figure 7.15.
1. What complaints are being made about Nike and other corporations?
2. Who are making the complaints?
3. How have the corporations responded?
4. What answers are suggested?
5. Use the Nike example to show how globalisation works and why corporations organise their business in this way. ➡

Review

- Within the past 50 years, Japan has become the world's second largest industrial nation.
- Japan's industry has gone through several phases of modernisation and diversification.
- The economies of countries such as Japan are 'hollowing out' as manufacturing moves to lower cost locations.
- Globalisation is one of the most powerful forces driving world industry today.
- Globalisation brings threats as well as benefits to people and nations.

Changing agriculture

CASE STUDY: Life in two great deltas: Ganges–Brahmaputra and Mekong

Main activity

Assessment of flood hazard management strategies.

Key ideas

● Deltas are zones of hazard as well as opportunity.
● Deltas need careful management.
● Deltas contain a combination of fertile soils and water which attract farming populations.

Do you know?

? That deltas are built by rivers carrying sediment into shallow coastal seas.
? That some of the highest population densities in the world are found in several large deltas in tropical regions.
? The importance of understanding how seasonal variations in river flow affect deltas and people living in them.
? That in a monsoon climate there is a distinct wet and dry season as in India.

Two great deltas

The Ganges–Brahmaputra and the Mekong rivers have built two of the largest deltas in the world (Figure 8.1). Both river basins have a monsoon climate (see Unit 2, page 17), and so river flows vary greatly through the year. Both deltas have population densities of over 800 per square kilometre, some of the highest in the world. Most people are farmers who depend upon the seasonal floods to irrigate their crops. It is these floodwaters which carry the sediment which builds the deltas, and makes the soils so fertile. Yet the images we see of the deltas on television and in newspapers are very different (Figures 8.2 and 8.3).

Figure 8.2: Flooding in Bangladesh

Figure 8.3: Fertile paddy fields in the Mekong Delta

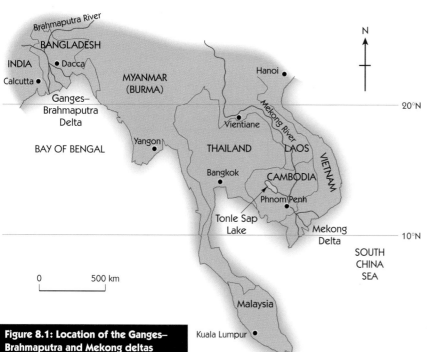
Figure 8.1: Location of the Ganges–Brahmaputra and Mekong deltas

▼ Questions

1 In which countries do the Ganges–Brahmaputra and Mekong deltas lie?
2 Give two reasons why these deltas can support so many farmers.
3 Explain why river flows from July to October are as much as ten times greater than those in winter.
4 Describe briefly the images shown in the two photographs (Figures 8.2 and 8.3).

Facing the floods in Bangladesh

Three-quarters of Bangladesh lies in the Ganges–Brahmaputra Delta (the Brahmaputra is called the River Jamuna in Bangladesh). Each summer the rivers flood across the flat delta land, and the farmers rely on these regular floods (Figure 8.4).

The problem for Bangladesh is that the floods vary from year to year. Every few years large floods destroy the chars (**levees**) and villages. The waters are too deep and last too long for

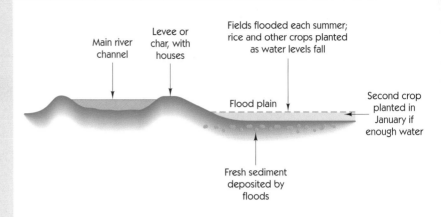

Figure 8.4: Normal flood conditions in the delta

farmers to plant their crops. This happened in 1974, 1988 and 1996. There are also violent tropical storms in the Bay of Bengal which cause tidal surges and flood many coastal areas (Figure 8.5).

The Bangladesh government has a massive Flood Action Plan (FAP) to try to control these disastrous floods. Almost 8000 kilometres of flood levees are being built along the main river channels. It is nearly completed and will cost at least £1.5 billion. Many people believe it will not work (Figure 8.6).

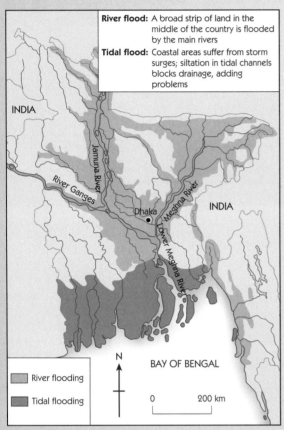

> **River flood:** A broad strip of land in the middle of the country is flooded by the main rivers
>
> **Tidal flood:** Coastal areas suffer from storm surges; siltation in tidal channels blocks drainage, adding problems

During the 1996 summer monsoon season, floods covered 50% of Bangladesh. At least 100 people were killed, 170,000 houses were destroyed and over 4000 cattle died. The 1988 flood disaster was much more severe. Three-quarters of the country was flooded and over 7 million houses were damaged or destroyed. There were serious food shortages the following year because rice production fell by 3 million tonnes.

Figure 8.5: Flooding in Bangladesh

Figure 8.6: Two views on flood control

Government water engineer

The natural river levees or chars are not high enough or strong enough to resist the major floods and so get washed away. Our stronger new embankments will let the floodwaters flow more quickly through the delta to the sea. We have gates in the banks and take-off canals to supply the farmers' fields with irrigation water. So, when the FAP is finished, we'll have floods where and when *we* want them.

Environmentalist

The FAP won't work. Look at the 1996 floods. Bangladesh already had 7000 kilometres of the new flood levees, but the rivers still flooded disastrously. The levees and straighter channels mean that the rivers flow more quickly and erode the banks more powerfully. Also, water arrives more quickly to areas without levees, so the flooding is greater. Don't forget, too, that less sediment will get to the fields to keep the soils fertile.

▼ Questions

5 Describe briefly the relationship between floods and farmers in Bangladesh.

6 Look carefully at Figure 8.5. Describe the distribution of flooding.

7 Explain the two types of flooding which cause problems in Bangladesh.

8 a Which type of flood is the FAP trying to control?
   b What methods are being used?
   c How may they help farmers?

9 Why does the environmentalist (Figure 8.6) believe the FAP will not work?

Success in the Mekong Delta

The Mekong Delta is densely populated. Villages lie along the natural levees and built dikes, and rice paddies cover much of the flat delta surface. As in the Ganges–Brahmaputra Delta, the farmers rely on floods caused by the summer monsoon rains. However, disastrous floods are rare. This is because the large Tonle Sap Lake acts as an emergency store for excess water (Figure 8.7). Also, there are few violent storms from the sea. So, the Vietnamese farmers have been more successful than the Bangladeshi farmers in modernising their agriculture.

Changes in the delta

The delta has four main parts (Figure 8.8). For hundreds of years, most people lived and farmed in areas I and II. During the past 30 years, this has changed because of:

● population growth – the population has doubled.
● diversification – farmers are growing more commercial crops.
● improved technology – new land has been drained for irrigation. Water storage schemes mean irrigation water is available all year.
● the 'green revolution' – new high yielding varieties of rice are being grown.

As a result, intensive farming has spread across the delta fringes (areas IV a, b) and commercial shrimp farming is expanding along the coast (area III). There has been a farming revolution.

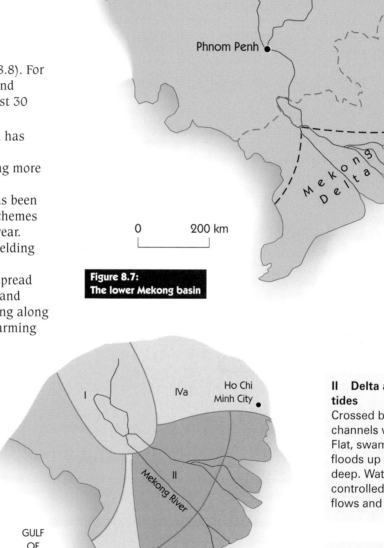

**Figure 8.7:
The lower Mekong basin**

I   Main delta floodplain
Two main river channels lined with levees. Floodplain is swampy and floods up to two metres deep. Water level controlled by seasonal river flows.

IV a and b   Delta fringes
Very flat and mostly less than one metre above sea level. Floods up to three metres deep. Poor water quality, and floods drain slowly.

II   Delta affected by tides
Crossed by marsh channels with low levees. Flat, swampy floodplain floods up to one metre deep. Water levels controlled by seasonal flows and daily tides.

III   Coastal margins
Crossed by low sandy ridges and mangrove swamps. Salt problems in the water, and floods up to 0.5 metres deep. Water level mainly controlled by tides.

Figure 8.8: The Mekong Delta

Figure 8.9 shows that farmers have changed from growing one rice crop a year during the flood season (i), to growing two (ii), three (iii) and even four (iv) crops a year. Not only do they sell more rice, but also a wider range of fruit and other food crops. The traditional methods relied upon the natural flood rhythms. Today, however, dams, canals and pumps make water available for irrigation through most of the year. The new high yielding varieties of rice grow and ripen more quickly than the traditional types.

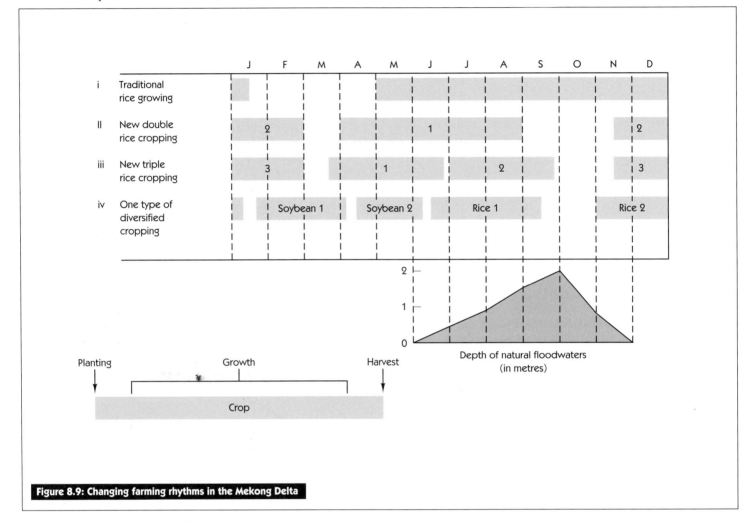

Figure 8.9: Changing farming rhythms in the Mekong Delta

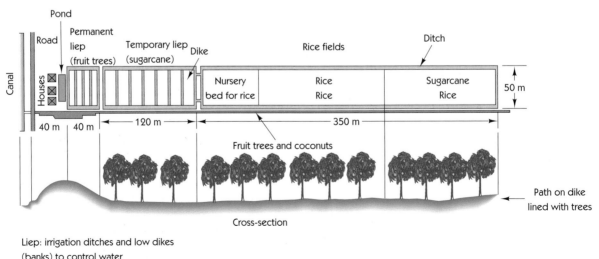

Liep: irrigation ditches and low dikes
(banks) to control water

Figure 8.10: An Yip's farm in the Mekong Delta

Three stages in a revolution

Not all farmers have changed, but families like An Yip's (Figure 8.10) have lived through three enormous changes during the past thirty years:
● before 1970: traditional farming – one crop of rice a year;
● 1970–85: intensification – using new rice varieties and year-round water to grow several crops a year;
● since 1985: diversification – adding several commercial crops to the rice farming.

Careful use of space and water

The plan of An Yip's fields shows how he can grow so much on his small farm (Figure 8.10). His is one of a long line of farms which run back from the canal. His father was a traditional rice farmer, but An Yip has diversified. Irrigation water can be pumped on to his fields all-year. He plants fast-growing rice to get two crops a year, and grows several other crops to sell.

▼ Questions

Use Figure 8.9.

10 Describe the traditional farmer's year (i) and how it related to the natural river floods. ➤

11 Use the chart to support the statement that the new varieties of rice grow and ripen more quickly than the traditional varieties. ➤

12 Explain how the chart tells us that farmers no longer have to rely on the natural seasonal floods.

Use Figure 8.10.

13 Describe the shape of the farm.

14 How far is it from the canal to the end of the farm?

15 What crops does An Yip grow?

16 Describe what you would see as you walk from the road, along the path to the end of the farm.

17 Use the three stages of the Mekong Delta's farming revolution to describe how life for An Yip's family has changed and improved during the past thirty years.

18 Compare and contrast the Ganges–Brahmaputra and Mekong deltas, using the following headings:
● Climate
● Seasonal river flows
● Landscape
● Type of agriculture
● Changes over the past 30 years
● Problems ➤

Review

● The large river deltas of Bangladesh and Vietnam are fertile areas with high population densities and intensive farming.
● Heavy summer monsoon rains over the river basins cause seasonal flooding across the deltas.
● Farmers rely on the floods but are also at risk because the floods vary in size from year to year.
● The Ganges–Brahmaputra Delta is more at risk from disastrous floods than the Mekong Delta.
● Flood control has been more successful in the Mekong Delta and so improvements in farming and quality of life have been better than in Bangladesh.

Do you know?

? Many people in LEDCs (Less Economically Developed countries) need greater access to land to be able to grow more crops both to feed themselves and to sell.

? Export earnings are vital for LEDCs so that they can obtain foreign currency to buy much needed imports.

? Irrigation is a valuable technique for increasing crop yield.

? Sustainable development means that improvements can be maintained over long periods of time.

CASE STUDY: More land, more water: Chile

Main activity

Analysing information to assess policies for changing land use.

Key ideas

● Development = economic growth + improved quality of life.
● In most LEDCs, agriculture is the mainstay of life and development, but needs modernising.

Key issues

Three related problems which must be solved if farming is to be modernised are:
1 access to land – is there land available for all who need it?
2 access to water – is water available to all farmers who need it?
3 access to markets – do farmers grow crops for which there is a demand, and can they reach these markets?

This case study shows how people in a farming valley in Chile have solved these problems.

Changes in Chile

In the mid-1960s, the majority of farmland in Chile was owned by the government or by rich families with large estates, or *fundias*. This meant that most families in rural areas had very small holdings, or no land at all. The population was increasing and there were strong campaigns for more land to be made available.

As a result, in 1967 the government passed a major Land Reform Act. The main aim was to provide many more family farms. This has been done by breaking up many of the large estates and by making government land available to small farmers. The success of the scheme is seen in the change in landholding patterns over 20 years (Figure 8.11).

As this land reform was happening, agriculture in Chile was also changing. Growing crops for export has become much more important. This has meant more money for thousands of farming families. However, much of the increased productivity has been based on irrigation, and scientists are becoming concerned that too much water is being used. There are doubts, therefore, about whether Chile's farming economic development is sustainable.

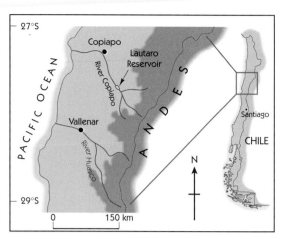

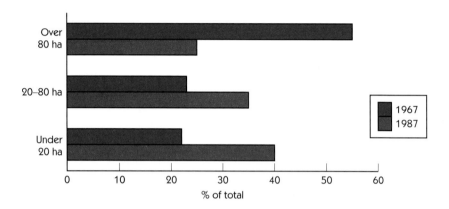

Figure 8.11: Farm sizes in Chile, 1967 and 1987 (% of total farmland)

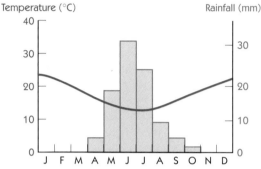

Figure 8.12: The physical background of the Copiapo area

The Upper Copiapo Valley

Environment

The River Copiapo rises in the Andes Mountains and flows west for 250 kilometres to the Pacific Ocean. It lies within the region known as Norte Chico, in the drier northern half of Chile (Figure 8.12). The local annual rainfall is only about 100 millimetres. It is unreliable and falls between April and August. However, the Copiapo flows permanently as it is fed by snow-melt from the High Andes. All the tributary streams are seasonal. These have cut deep ravines which drop into the flat floor of the main valley (Figure 8.13). Today the flow is controlled by the Lautaro Dam. This is important, as all crops rely on irrigation.

Land reform

Land reform began in the Copiapo Valley in 1978:
● Farmers with less than 80 hectares were allowed to keep their farms.
● The original owners of larger farms were each allowed to keep 80 hectares, and a further 50 hectares for each son under 21 years of age.
● The remaining area of almost 1000 hectares was divided into farms with an average size of 25 hectares.
● These new farms were given to families, many of whom were from other parts of Chile. Because these people were not very attached to the local land, some sold to richer commercial farmers.
● Not all the land went to small farmers. The government sold over 1500 fertile hectares to private companies or rich individuals.

Figure 8.13: The Copiapo Valley

Agricultural change

There have been two other important changes in the Upper Copiapo Valley. First, the area under cultivation has almost trebled. Second, different commercial crops are grown for different markets. The scale of these changes is shown clearly by the figures (Figure 8.14) and the land use maps (Figure 8.15). Until 1980, cereals, vegetables, fruit and meat were sold mainly to Santiago (the capital of Chile) and other cities.

Today, the farmland is mainly vineyards, and the grapes are exported, particularly to the USA, which buys 55% of all Chile's grapes. Picking and packing the grapes in November and December is labour intensive. There are too few people in Copiapo's small towns and villages, so up to 1500 seasonal workers are brought in. Costs are kept down because wages are only one-tenth of those in the European Union or USA.

Land use	1965	1985	1995
Annual crops (cereals, fruit, vegetables) and improved grassland	1340	720	720
Fruit trees	75	70	60
Vineyards	225	3300	4000
Total	*1670*	*4090*	*4760*

Figure 8.14: Land use changes in the Upper Copiapo Valley, 1965–95 (hectares)

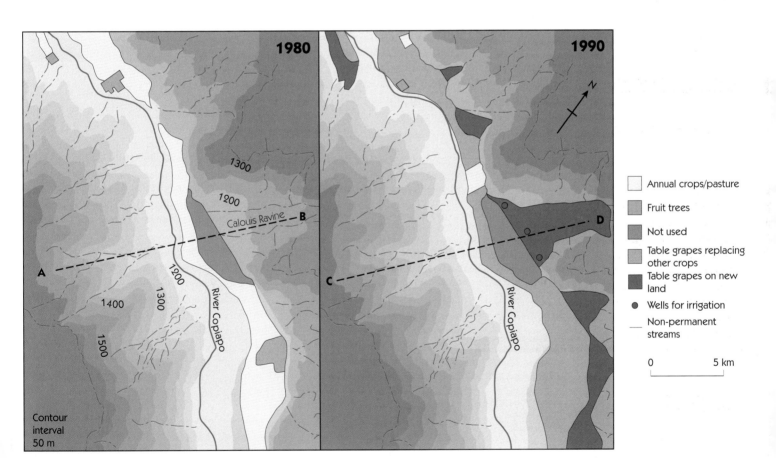

Figure 8.15: Land use changes in the Copiapo Valley

▼ Questions

1. From the data in Figure 8.14, construct pie charts for each of the three years. Use a scale of one centimetre radius = 1000 hectares to decide the size of your circles. Divide the circles according to the proportion of the total area given over to each land use type.

2. What percentage of the total crop land was under vineyards in (a) 1965 and (b) 1995?

3. In one sentence, sum up the changes in land use over the 30 years.

4. From the land use maps of Figure 8.15:
   a. Draw two cross-sections along lines A–B (1980) and C–D (1990). Label the features and land use.
   b. Use your cross-sections, the maps and the photo (Figure 8.13) to describe the physical landscape of the Upper Copiapo Valley. (Look carefully at the valley floor and valley sides.)
   c. Describe the changes in land use type and location between 1980 and 1990.

5. Why was economic development needed in the Copiapo Valley, and how has it been achieved? ➡

The power of water

The rapid expansion of vineyards has happened in two ways. First, farmers have planted vines on their existing land. Second, new land has been brought into cultivation. This can be seen by comparing the two maps of Figure 8.15. Farming has become more intensive and covers a much larger area. As all vines must be irrigated in this hot, semi-arid climate, water demand has trebled. Two local people explain how the system works.

The traditional method of gravity canals is still the best on the flat valley floor. They take off water from the river and run through the field systems. Each farmer uses sluice gates in the canal banks or pumps to direct water on to his crops. The grape vines use much more water than cereals and vegetables, but so far we have been OK because of the Lautaro Dam. Also, more farmers are using efficient drip-feed pipe systems. Small holes in the pipes drop water at the plant base and very little is wasted.

Figure 8.16: Ramon Zepeda, water resources engineer

The gravity canals work fine on the valley floor, but can't reach the higher land at the mouths of the ravines. This is why these fertile soils were not used. But today, this is where I have my 20 hectares of new grape vines. Things are different because we get good prices for our grapes. This means we can afford to pump water up on to the higher land, and sink wells into the sediments. These sediments hold water, that is they are good aquifers. But, this modern equipment is expensive to put in. This has meant that richer farmers and commercial companies are buying out smaller farmers. I've managed by taking a loan from the fruit packing corporation which buys my grapes.

Figure 8.17: Alfonso Pessenti, farmer

Is the growth sustainable?

Land reform + a new high quality attractive crop + modern technology = successful development for the people of the Copiapo Valley. But can this success be sustained? Three question marks hang over the future:

● Average annual rainfall of the Norte Chico region has declined by 30% during the twentieth century. **Global warming** is likely to cause a further fall. So, will water shortages limit the growth of the economy?

● As the agriculture becomes more 'high tech', richer farmers and companies are buying out smaller farmers. Might this mean that there will be more landless people once more?

● Farming in the Copiapo and other valleys of the Norte Chico region has become heavily dependent upon a single crop – grapes. Is this **monoculture** dangerous? For example, what if another competitor takes over the US market, or a plant disease affects the Chilean vines?

▼ Questions

6. What is meant by a 'gravity canal' system and why does it work only across the valley floor? (You may find a labelled diagram useful.)

7. Look at Figure 8.17. Describe how water is brought to new areas and explain why it has been possible.

8. Why does Alfonso Pessenti think that land reform is not working well? (Think of the aim of land reform, and then of what is happening.)

9. Suggest three reasons why the Copiapo Valley has so far not suffered a shortage of irrigation water.

10. Most of the Copiapo farmers belong to a local co-operative association. At one of their meetings, they discuss the three questions hanging over their future. For each of the questions, suggest one proposal they could put forward to try to answer the problem. ➡

Review

● The Copiapo Valley example shows the importance of land reform in improving the quality of life of rural communities.
● There are difficulties in achieving sustainable development.

Changing populations

CASE STUDY: International migration: South Africa

Migration and South Africa

Today, at least 125 million people in the world live outside the country where they were born. They are **international migrants**. They have emigrated for many reasons. For example, around 20 million are refugees, that is, people who have been forced to move from their homelands. In order to understand migration, we need to ask several questions:

● How many people migrate?
● What type of people migrate?
● Where do they move from and to?
● Why do they move?

The information in this case study helps you to answer these questions for one country. South Africa is one of the largest countries in Africa, and one of the richest (Figure 9.1). Yet there are extremes of wealth and poverty. The majority of the population are Black Africans. Yet only since 1994 have they had the same rights to vote as the White minority. These rights were won after many years of conflict. The figures in this case study cover some of these years of conflict and rapid change in South Africa.

Using information to answer questions

Figure 9.2 gives us the information to answer questions about how many people are moving in and out of South Africa.

Main activity

Enquiry based on population data analysis.

Key ideas

● People migrate into and out of a country for different reasons.
● Migration patterns for a country vary over time.

Do you know?

❓ Net migration for a country is the balance between immigration (arrivals) and emigration (departures).
❓ People migrate for different reasons, either because they want to, or because they feel they have to.
❓ There are 'push' and 'pull' factors which affect migration.

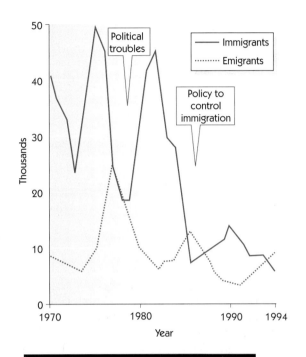

Figure 9.2: Immigration to and emigration from South Africa since 1970

Figure 9.1: South Africa – location

FACTFILE: South Africa

Area	1.2 million square kilometres
Location	Southern tip of the African continent
Population	41 million – 76% are Black Africans, 13% have European origins; 50% live in urban areas
Main cities	Pretoria (capital) 1.1 million; Cape Town 2.4 million; Johannesburg 2.0 million
Population growth rate	0.8% a year
Education	82% of the people are literate
Health	70% have access to a safe water supply
Land use (% of total area)	Crops 11%; pasture 67%; other uses 22%
Economy	World's largest producer of gold and diamonds and second largest producer of manganese; a range of modern industries

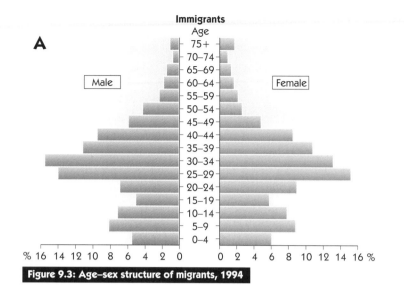

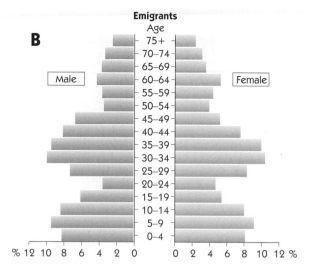

Figure 9.3: Age–sex structure of migrants, 1994

▼ Questions

Study Figure 9.2.

1 In which years were there (a) the most, (b) the fewest immigrants to South Africa?

2 Migration varies greatly from year to year. Give the highest and lowest annual totals for (a) immigration, (b) emigration.

3 It is important to know whether more people are moving in (immigrants) than are leaving (emigrants). For example, the graphs show that in 1980 there were approximately 30,000 immigrants and 10,000 emigrants. This gave a **net migration balance** of +20,000. During which years was there a negative net migration balance, that is, more emigrants than immigrants?

4 Describe the changing pattern of migration for South Africa during the period 1970–90.

Study Figure 9.3.

5 Who moves? The age–sex pyramid graphs divide migrants into five-year age groups. Each bar shows the percentage of male and female immigrants or emigrants in each age group. So, in Figure 9.3A, 5.8% of male immigrants in 1994 were aged 0–4 years.

a What is the most popular age for (a) male and (b) female immigrants?

b What proportion of total (a) male and (b) female immigrants are aged between 25 and 44 years?

c Describe the pattern of immigration into South Africa during 1994. You may find it useful to base your description on four phases: 1. Children (0–14 years); 2. Young adults (15–24); 3. Middle adults (25–44); 4. Mature and elderly (45 and older).

d Explain how the age–sex pyramid supports this statement: 'One important group of immigrants are families with children of school age'. ➡

e What proportion of (a) male and (b) female emigrants fall into these age phases: (i) 0–14 years; (ii) 25–44 years; (iii) 55 and older?

f Explain how the age–sex pyramid supports this statement: 'The two largest groups of emigrants are families with children, and people leaving after they retire'. ➡

g Compare and contrast the immigration and emigration age–sex pyramids. ➡

Many people move to improve their quality of life. This includes the hope of getting a job or a better job. Like all countries, South Africa has a policy to control the number and type of immigrants. The South African government is trying to attract people with good educational and job skills. In contrast, it is restricting the numbers of lower skilled workers. This policy is one factor which influences the figures in the immigration column of Figure 9.4.

Occupation	Immigrants	Emigrants
Professionals and managers	62	53
Clerical workers	15	21
Industrial workers, including mining	10	10
Other services	5	3
Other occupations	8	13
Total number	*6000*	*9000*

Figure 9.4: The occupations of migrants in 1994 (% of total)

In democratic countries such as South Africa, there are few controls on emigration. In 1994, a completely new type of government was being elected. So, many people were worried about what would happen. This helps to explain why emigration grew to 9000 in that year (Figure 9.4, last column).

Origins and destinations of migrants

The information in Figures 9.5 and 9.6 allow us to answer questions about where people come from and move to.

The pie charts show how quickly migration patterns can change. Notice that the total numbers of immigrants for 1994 are much lower than in 1984.

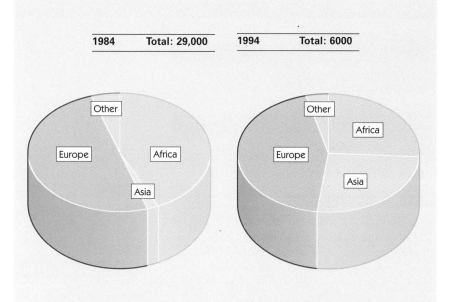

Main countries in 1994 (% of total from that continent)

From Europe:		From Asia:		From Africa:	
United Kingdom	38%	China	35%	Zimbabwe	34%
Former Yugoslavia	12%	India	28%	Zaire	15%

Figure 9.5: Where immigrants came from in 1984 and 1994

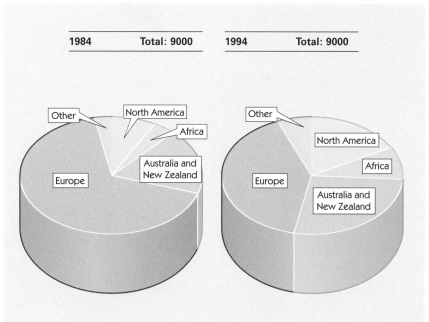

Main countries in 1994 (numbers)

United Kingdom	2900	Australia	1300
New Zealand	1500	Canada	1000

Figure 9.6: Where emigrants went in 1984 and 1994

Main activity

Analysis of population data.

Key ideas

● Economic opportunity is a powerful factor influencing migration.

China, a moving giant

More than 1.2 billion people live in China. This is almost one-quarter of the world's population. In addition, many millions of Chinese live in other countries (Figure 9.7). Much larger numbers are moving within China. In 1995, at least 105 million people were living in a different province from that in which they were born. This huge migration has occurred mainly since 1984, when the communist government began to allow people to move more freely. It is especially the young people who migrate (Figure 9.8).

'Push' factors: At least four out of every ten migrants have moved from rural to urban areas. China's population is growing by 15 million a year, while agricultural land is decreasing. In 1965 the arable farm land covered 110 million hectares. In 1995 this had fallen to 95 million hectares. We can sum up the problem as an equation:

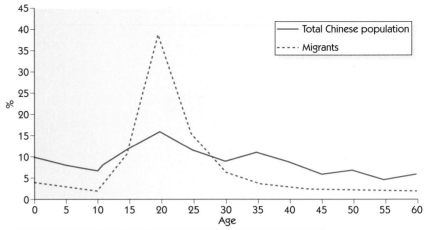

Figure 9.8: Age structure of rural–urban migrants in China, 1990

$$\left.\begin{array}{l}\text{Population growth}\\\text{Reduced arable land}\\\text{Modernisation of farming}\\\text{Few job opportunities}\end{array}\right\} = \begin{array}{l}\text{many people without}\\\text{land, jobs or income}\\\text{in rural areas}\end{array}$$

'Pull' factors: China's cities and industries are growing rapidly, especially in provinces of eastern China. Here, the government is encouraging industries in Special Economic Zones, e.g. around the huge cities of Shanghai and Hong Kong. The construction, manufacturing and service industries together create several million new jobs every year. So:

$$\left.\begin{array}{l}\text{New industries}\\\text{More jobs}\\\text{Higher wages}\\\text{More housing}\end{array}\right\} = \begin{array}{l}\text{growing demand}\\\text{for workers}\\\text{in cities}\end{array}$$

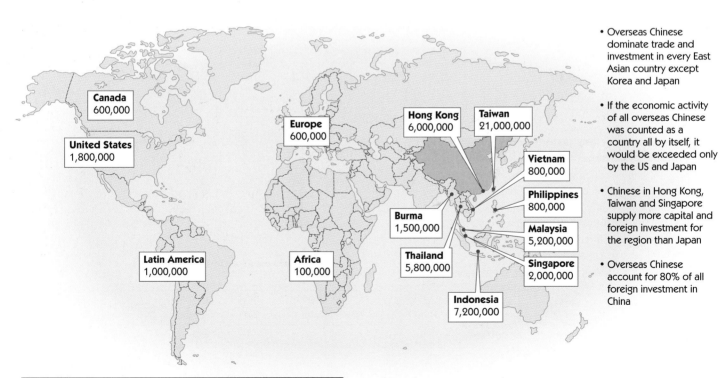

- Overseas Chinese dominate trade and investment in every East Asian country except Korea and Japan

- If the economic activity of all overseas Chinese was counted as a country all by itself, it would be exceeded only by the US and Japan

- Chinese in Hong Kong, Taiwan and Singapore supply more capital and foreign investment for the region than Japan

- Overseas Chinese account for 80% of all foreign investment in China

Figure 9.7: Numbers of ethnic Chinese living outside mainland China

Migration in China: The story of Yua Chen

Yua Chen and her husband, Lo, live in the city of Guilin, in Guangxi Province, South East China. He has a job in an electronics factory, packing computer components for export. She collects cardboard and bottles, to sell to a merchant. Like 40% of the 150,000 people who live in Guilin, Yua Chen and Lo have migrated from farming villages. There are more jobs and they can earn more money in the city. Now that the Chinese government allows people to run their own businesses, they are saving to open a shop.

Figure 9.9: Yua Chen at work

Figure 9.10: Yua Chen's village

Yua Chen and Lo came from this village in Sichuan Province in 1993. Each family has less than one hectare of land, and the population is growing. Almost all of the woodland has gone, and fields and terraces use most of the land. When Lo's father died, his elder brother took over the family field. Lo had no land and there were few other jobs in the village. Yua Chen and Lo had heard about all the industries, construction, jobs and higher wages in the cities. So, after they married, they moved 800 kilometres south east to Guilin.

Yua Chen, Lo and their baby daughter live in two tiny rooms in one of these old houses. They are hoping for a flat in one of the many large blocks being built by the Guilin council. However, there is a problem. Yua Chen and Lo are not 'official' migrants. That is, they did not get a government permit to leave their village. This means that until the Guilin council accepts them as 'official' residents, they cannot get on to the housing waiting list. The majority of the over 100 million migrants in China are, like Yua Chen and Lo, unofficial migrants.

Figure 9.11: Yua Chen's home

China's shifting population

Yua Chen and Lo are only two of over 2 million people who have left Sichuan Province in central China since 1985. Sichuan is a mainly agricultural region, with growing population pressure on the land. Figure 9.14 shows how many people migrated between 1985 and 1990. Most of the migrants went to cities in the rapidly growing provinces to the east and south. Figure 9.12 is a list of the six most popular provinces.

Province	Number
Guangdong	200,000
Hubei	150,000
Guizhou	150,000
Yunnan	140,000
Fujian	100,000
Jiangsu	100,000

Figure 9.12: Popular destinations for Sichuan migrants, 1985–90

Figure 9.13: The provinces of China

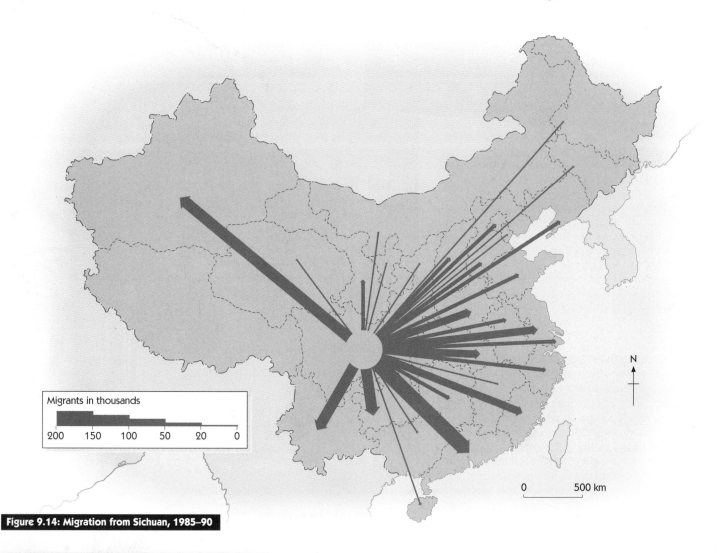

Migrants in thousands
200 150 100 50 20 0

Figure 9.14: Migration from Sichuan, 1985–90

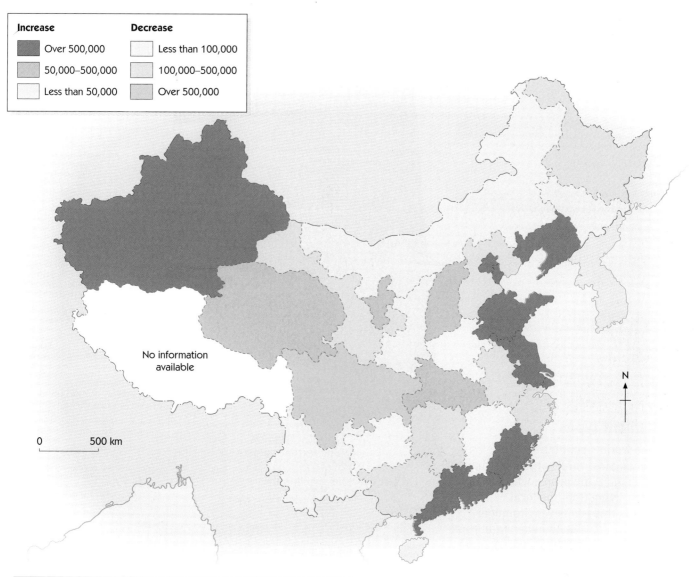

Increase

■ (dark)	Over 500,000
▨ (mid grey)	50,000–500,000
□ (white)	Less than 50,000

Decrease

□ (white)	Less than 100,000
▨ (light grey)	100,000–500,000
▨ (grey)	Over 500,000

No information available

0   500 km

N

Figure 9.15: Population change caused by internal migration, 1985–90

▼ Questions

1 What factors (a) 'pushed' Yua Chen and Lo from Sichuan and (b) 'pulled' them to Guilin?

2 Why are they classed as 'unofficial' migrants and how is this a problem for them?

3 Study Figures 9.12, 9.13 and 9.14. Which of the provinces in Figure 9.12 are (a) nearest to Sichuan, or (b) along China's east coast? Use your answers to support these ideas:
- Most migration within a country is over relatively short distances.
- People move to areas where jobs and wages are growing most rapidly.

4 Study Figure 9.15.
a Name the three provinces which lost most people by migration.
b Name three provinces which gained large numbers of migrants.

5 From the information in this case study, write a brief report which describes and explains the pattern of recent migration in China. ➡

Review

● International migration in and out of South Africa is constantly changing. The number and type of migrants is affected by political conditions, job opportunities and government policy. Some factors attract people ('pull' factors) and some encourage people to leave ('push' factors).
● Internal migration in China is mainly from rural to urban areas and can be explained by 'push' and 'pull' factors.
● Most migration within China is either to neighbouring provinces or to the industrialising regions along the east coast.
● Most migrants are in the younger age groups.

10

Rural settlements

Rural settlement types

One-half of the world's population still lives in rural settlements. Most rural settlements have one thing in common: the people who live in them make their living from the local environment. It is this people–environment relationship which helps us to understand rural settlement patterns. Figures 10.1 and 10.2 are examples of this relationship at work. Look carefully at the photographs and we can describe the two settlements:

● The Chinese village is a cluster of buildings located between a river and a line of hills.
● The Navajo settlement consists of two buildings for one family, built at the foot of a long plateau.

However, if we are asked to explain these settlement types, then we need to understand the way the people use their environments.

The Chinese village and the Navajo homestead are examples of the two main types of rural settlement patterns found throughout the world:

● Nucleated – where varying numbers of families cluster together in village communities;
● Dispersed – where individual family homes are scattered across the landscape.

The case studies in this unit use maps rather than photographs to show that nucleated settlements develop in contrasting environments in very different parts of the world.

Figure 10.1: A village along the River Li in China

Paths lead from the village to small fields and terraces where villagers grow food crops. The river provides fish and the main travel route. The 20 families can support themselves from a small area and so are able to live in a nucleated settlement.

This environment is too dry for growing crops. The Navajo are sheep farmers and, to find enough grazing, the animals roam across wide areas. As each family needs to be near to their flocks, the family hogans are scattered across the landscape. This is a dispersed settlement pattern.

Figure 10.2: A Navajo hogan (six-sided house) in Arizona, USA

What can maps tell us?

A map gives us a view looking directly down on a place. However, it is not a vertical air photograph. A map uses symbols, shading and labels to tell us about the place. This is why it is so useful to be able to 'read' a map; it is a source of information if we understand the language. The 'dictionary' for this language lies in the **scale** and the **symbols key**.

The two maps in this unit are of rural settlements in two tropical countries: Mauritius and The Gambia. They both show farming villages surrounded by field systems where most of the villagers make their living. As you 'read' these maps, you will learn something about the landscapes and the lives of the local people. Notice, too, how maps from different countries differ.

CASE STUDY: Learning from maps – Mauritius

FACTFILE: Mauritius

Area	An island of 1860 square kilometres
Size	53 kilometres E–W; 72 kilometres N–S
Location	Indian Ocean, 800 kilometres east of Madagascar
Population	1–2 million – 60% rural; 70% of Indo–Pakistani origin
Land use	Crops 52%; pasture 4%; woodland and settlement 44%
Main export	Sugar

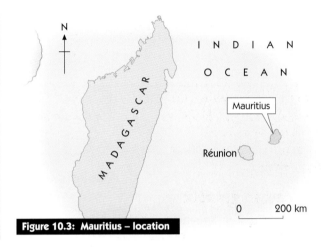

Figure 10.3: Mauritius – location

Figure 10.4: Mauritius – rural landscape

1. What is the scale of the map in Figure 10.5?
2. What are (a) the N–S and (b) the E–W distances across this map in kilometres?
3. If you lived at the farm at Bois Rouge, how far would you have to travel to the nearest school?
4. What is the contour interval of this map?
5. What is the approximate difference in altitude between the highest and lowest points?
6. In which general direction does the land slope downwards?
7. Describe the location and shape of the two villages: (a) Aussailles, (b) Gowsal.
8. Make a list of the buildings other than houses that these two communities have.
9. What are the two religions which seem important to the local people?
10. Mauritius is now an independent country. It was once a British colony, but what evidence is there that other countries have influenced the island?
11. What does the map tell us about the land use in this area?
12. Field boundaries are marked as 'sugar cane tracks'. These are the tracks used to haul the cut sugar to the factories. Describe the shape, size and pattern of these fields.
13. What does the map tell us about the drainage and water supply?
14. What jobs and professions are the local people likely to have? (Look carefully at the information on the map.)

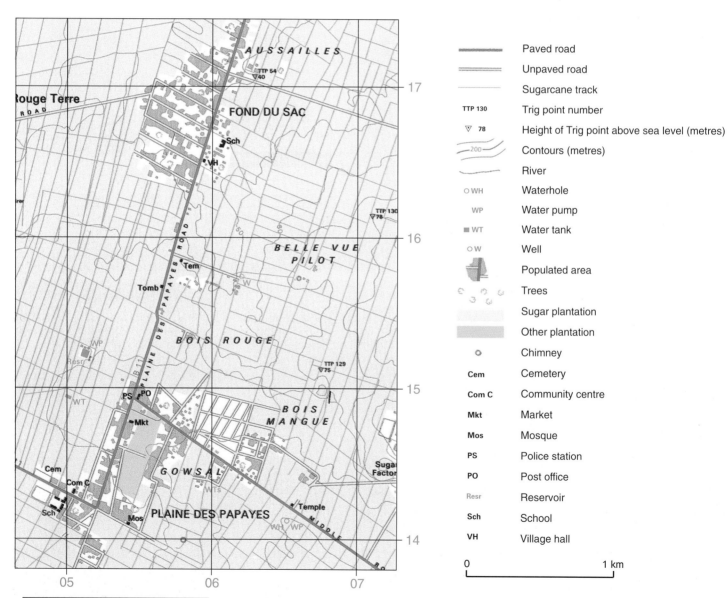

Figure 10.5: Linear village in Mauritius

FACTFILE: The Gambia

Area	11,300 square kilometres
Size	A 320-kilometre E–W strip along the Gambia River
Location	West Africa
Population	1.1 million; 75% rural; most people are Muslims; growth 2.4% a year
Land use	Crops 20%; pasture 10%; forest, savanna and settlement 70%
Main economic activities	Peanut exports and tourism

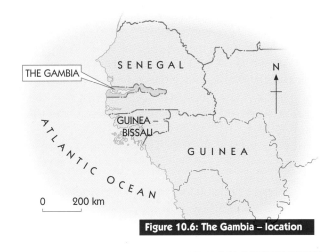

Figure 10.6: The Gambia – location

Figure 10.7: The Gambia – rural landscape

▼ Questions

1 What is the scale of the map in Figure 10.8?
2 What is the contour interval?
3 What area does the map cover in square kilometres?
4 If you walk at five kilometres per hour, how long would it take you to walk along the road across the map?
5 In which grid square of the map is the highest land found?
6 a Draw a cross-section from the NE to SW corners of the map
  b Label your cross-section to show (i) Sifoe village, (ii) the vegetation and land use types, (iii) the stream.
7 Use your cross-section and the shape of the contours to (a) describe the location of Sifoe village, (b) explain this location.

8 Give a brief description of Sifoe. You should include size, shape, street pattern, how the buildings are distributed, what facilities are mentioned.
9 Describe as carefully as you can what you would see if you walked along the road from south west to north east.
10 Why do you think that the villagers' fields, except for the rice paddies, are close to the village?
11 Explain the location of the rice paddies.
12 Describe the pattern of tracks across the map, and suggest the main reason for this pattern.
13 The local population is growing rapidly. In which direction do you think the village will grow? Why?

Review

● Maps are valuable sources of detailed information.

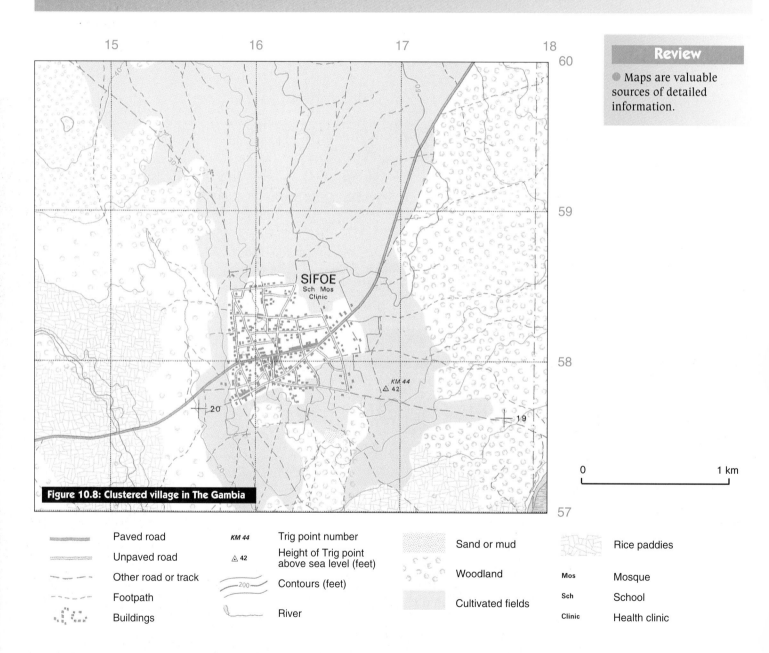

Figure 10.8: Clustered village in The Gambia

───── Paved road	*KM 44*	Trig point number	∷∷∷	Sand or mud	▨ Rice paddies
───── Unpaved road	△ 42	Height of Trig point above sea level (feet)	○○○	Woodland	**Mos** Mosque
─ ─ ─ Other road or track	⌇200⌇	Contours (feet)	▨	Cultivated fields	**Sch** School
- - - Footpath	⌇	River			**Clinic** Health clinic
⸱⸱⸱ Buildings					

0 ─────── 1 km

11

Changing cities

Key ideas

● A small but growing number of huge 'world cities', or metropolises, have distinct characteristics.

● There are strong social and economic contrasts between the inner core areas and the peripheries of metropolises.

● Core–periphery relationships are changing, to produce a new type of urban structure.

Do you know?

? The distribution of megacities across the world.

? About land use zoning patterns within large cities, e.g. the distribution of industry and housing; where different social groups live.

? The outward movement of jobs and people from inner cities to outer suburbs.

Main activity

Map and data interpretation.

The growth of megacities

For many years, atlases and books have included maps of 'millionaire' cities: metropolises with a population of at least 1 million. Today, we think in terms of 'megacities': huge urban concentrations with at least 10 million people. There are more than 20 of these megacities, or 'world cities'. They are found in the developing world, e.g. Mexico City, and in the developed world, e.g. New York Metropolitan Area (Figure 11.1).

Many millionaire cities which are expanding to become megacities have developed with a **metropolitan core**, surrounded by a suburban **periphery**. This is called a monocentric structure (Figure 11.2A). This produces a powerful radial commuter flow to and from the business core.

Figure 11.1: Satellite image of New York City (the area is approximately that shown on the inset map of Figure 11.4)

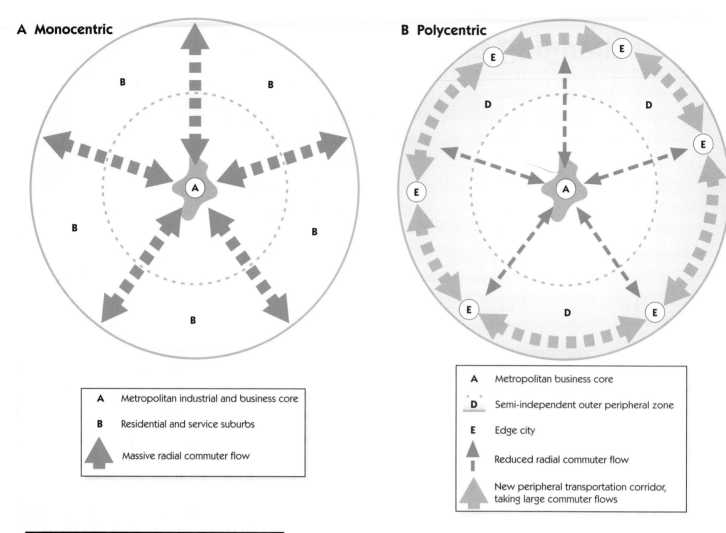

A Monocentric

B   B

B

A

B   B

B

A	Metropolitan industrial and business core
B	Residential and service suburbs
▲	Massive radial commuter flow

B Polycentric

E   E

D   D

E

E

A

E   D   E

A	Metropolitan business core
D	Semi-independent outer peripheral zone
E	Edge city
▲	Reduced radial commuter flow
▲	New peripheral transportation corridor, taking large commuter flows

Figure 11.2: Simple functional models for megacities

This pattern is changing:
● Industry has moved out of the core, which is increasingly concerned with professional and financial business.
● Wealthier families move to the suburbs; poorer families, and often ethnic minorities, are more likely to remain in the metropolitan core.
● New industries locate around the periphery in attractive environments (Figure 11.3).

The result is a polycentric structure (Figure 11.2B). A series of 'edge cities' grow around the periphery. Each has its own industries, businesses and services, which provide jobs for people living in the suburbs. Connections between the core and periphery weaken; links between the edge cities strengthen. This case study focuses on the question: 'Is the New York Metropolitan Area (called here, Greater New York) a polycentric megacity?'

Figure 11.3: A modern business complex

Are people moving?

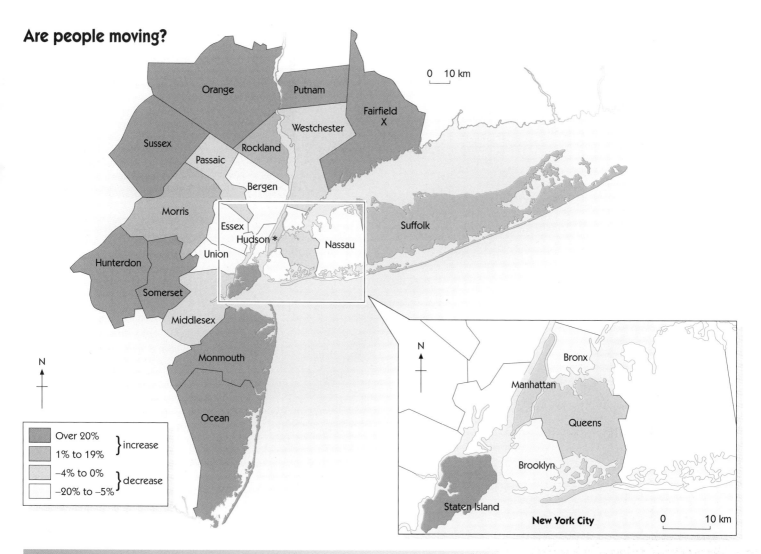

Figure 11.4: Population change in Greater New York, 1970–90 (the last census was taken in 1990)

▼ Questions

Use Figure 11.4.

1 Name two of the counties or boroughs with the most serious population decline. Are they in the core or the periphery of Greater New York?

2 Name two of the counties or boroughs which grew most rapidly. Are they in the core or the periphery?

3 Test this hypothesis: 'There is a relationship between population change and distance from the metropolitan centre.' Use this technique:

a On Figure 11.4, ✳ marks the metropolitan centre, on Manhattan Island. For each of the 24 units (boroughs and counties), locate a midpoint (X is an example for Fairfield County).

b Measure the straight-line centimetre distance from Manhattan to each of your midpoints.

c Construct the relationship graph below (use a computer graphics package if available). Plot your measured distances against population change on the graph (the first three have been done for you).

d Use the map and your graph to discuss the hypothesis.

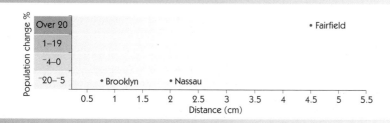

FACTFILE: Greater New York

● Greater New York has a population of about 18 million. This total has not changed greatly during the past 25 years.

● There are 24 political units – boroughs and counties.

● The metropolitan core is New York City, made up of five boroughs: Bronx, Brooklyn, Manhattan, Queens, Staten Island.

● The periphery is divided into 19 counties.

● The term 'Greater New York' is used to cover the whole megacity. This avoids confusion with the 'metropolitan core'.

What is happening to commuting?

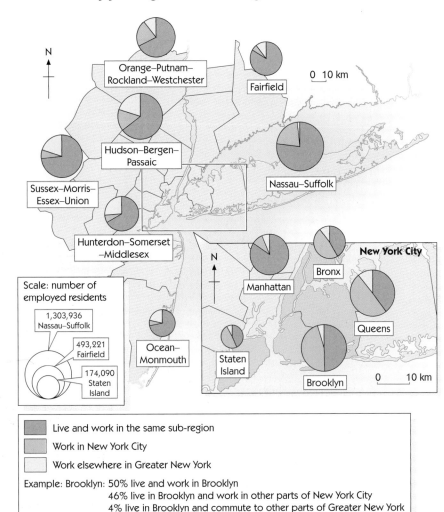

Scale: number of employed residents

1,303,936 Nassau–Suffolk

493,221 Fairfield

174,090 Staten Island

Live and work in the same sub-region

Work in New York City

Work elsewhere in Greater New York

Example: Brooklyn: 50% live and work in Brooklyn
46% live in Brooklyn and work in other parts of New York City
4% live in Brooklyn and commute to other parts of Greater New York

Notice that the 24 units are grouped into 12 sub-regions, with a pie chart for each. The five New York City boroughs make up the core, and the seven county groupings are the periphery.

Figure 11.5: Home–work relationships in Greater New York, 1990

We often hear that big city lifestyles have a 'work in the city – live in the suburbs' pattern. This is the monocentric system at work (Figure 11.2A): people commute from periphery to core and back again. But do megacities still fit this model? Figure 11.5 connects where people live with where they work in Greater New York.

A polycentric megacity (Figure 11.2B) includes these features:
● An inner business core, with many job opportunities (Figure 11.6).
● A series of edge cities around the periphery. These are not just residential suburbs; each has its own industrial, business and service centres, with many jobs.
● A new transportation corridor links these edge cities. This allows more commuting within and between the peripheral sub-regions. In turn, commuting to and from the core is reduced.

Figure 11.6: Manhattan Island

▼ Questions

Study Figure 11.5.

4 Describe, in one sentence, the main difference between Manhattan and the other four boroughs of New York City.

5 Manhattan Island is the centre for financial business and headquarters offices of big corporations. It also has many expensive apartment blocks. Suggest how this helps to explain the pie chart for Manhattan borough.

6 a Construct a table for the seven sub-regions of the periphery to include:
  ● name of sub-region;
  ● total number of employed residents (use the scale for the proportional circles showing the number of employed residents to give an approximate figure);
  ● % who work in their own sub-region;
  ● % who commute to New York City.

  b Approximately how many people commute from the periphery to the New York City core, and what percentage of total workers is this?

7 From Figure 11.5 and your table (see question 6a above), what evidence is there that Greater New York is developing a polycentric structure?

8 a Define the term 'megacity'.
  b What is meant by an 'edge city'?
  c Give three important features of a monocentric metropolis.
  d Use the case study of Greater New York to illustrate how the continued outward movement of people and jobs can result in the emergence of a polycentric megacity. ➡

Review

● A growing number of huge 'world cities' or megacities are emerging.
● Metropolises continue to expand as people and jobs move outwards.
● Commuting remains a problem in metropolises.
● An edge city is economically and socially semi-independent of the metropolitan core.
● Megacities are developing a polycentric structure.

The issue

As the case study of Greater New York shows, world cities expand outwards. Not all have the space to continue to do so. Other options are to grow upwards and inwards. There is also the prestige of being located in the 'downtown' districts. No city illustrates these processes more vividly than Hong Kong. Almost 7 million people live here, at some of the highest population densities in the world. Because Hong Kong is such a rich and prosperous city, there is great pressure for further growth and development. One plan is to fill in part of the famous Victoria Harbour around which the central city has been built, but there is strong opposition. This case study puts the case for and against the plan.

As Figure 11.7 shows, Hong Kong is a megacity with a serious space problem. The businesses and people of one of the richest economies in the world are crowded into an area about the size of London. However, Hong Kong is growing more rapidly than London – more people; more businesses; more trade. The remaining space is either marshland or steep, rocky hills, which is difficult to develop. As a result, the government has had to face two key questions (Figure 11.8).

Figure 11.7: Central Hong Kong

Where do we find the economic space for new businesses and to sustain economic growth?

Where can we find the living space which will improve the quality of life for Hong Kong people?

Figure 11.8: Finding economic and living space

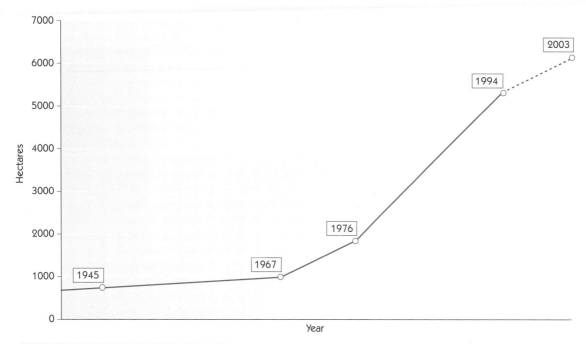

Figure 11.9: Reclaimed land in Hong Kong

The story so far

One answer has been to allow very high densities for housing and businesses. The other answer has been to make more space available by **land reclamation** (Figure 11.9). This means:
● infilling shallow coastal waters;
● draining low-lying marshes and irrigated farmland.

Figure 11.11 explains how the land reclamation programme has worked. Notice the two different approaches: first, dispersal – spreading development across the New Territories; second, concentration – intensifying development within the core city. It is this second policy, which causes much coastal infilling (Figure 11.10), which is arousing so much opposition.

Assessing the land reclamation plans

The present land reclamation plans include three main areas (Figure 11.11): the new airport west of Lantau Island (III); the massive container port developments between Kowloon and Lantau Island (II); the central city core around Victoria Harbour (I). It is the Victoria Harbour projects (Figure 11.13) which are causing the strongest opposition.

Figure 11.10: Continuing infilling and reclamation of Victoria Harbour

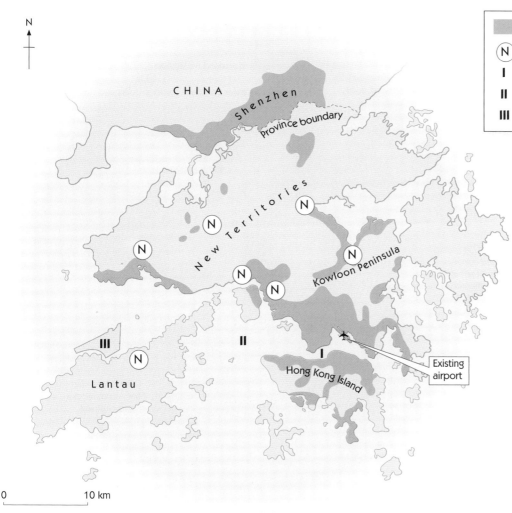

CHINA

Shenzhen

Province boundary

New Territories

Kowloon Peninsula

Lantau

Hong Kong Island

Existing airport

0   10 km

Phase 1: 1970–85 – decentralisation

More than 3000 hectares of lowland and coastal fringe in the New Territories have been reclaimed. On this land, a series of new towns has been built, with homes for 2.5 million people, plus industries and services. The idea has been to disperse people and economic activity away from the harbour area.

Phase 2: From 1985 – re-centralisation

This involves large-scale infilling along the fringes of Victoria Harbour and the shallow waters westwards towards Lantau Island. The schemes include port facilities, financial business developments, a new airport with its infrastructure, and housing projects.

Figure 11.11: Urban growth in Hong Kong

Figure 11.12: Sha Tin New Town – dispersal policy at work. Half a million people live in apartments in tower blocks. An efficient rail service links Sha Tin and the other new towns to central Hong Kong.

▼ Questions

Study Figure 11.11.

1 What are the approximate E–W and N–S distances across Hong Kong province?

2 Describe the distribution of urban growth.

3 The huge new airport opened in 1998. Suggest two reasons why Hong Kong needed to build this expensive facility.

4 Hong Kong is divided by water into several parts. Discuss the advantages and disadvantages of the physical setting of Hong Kong (look also at the photographs 11.10 and 11.12).➪

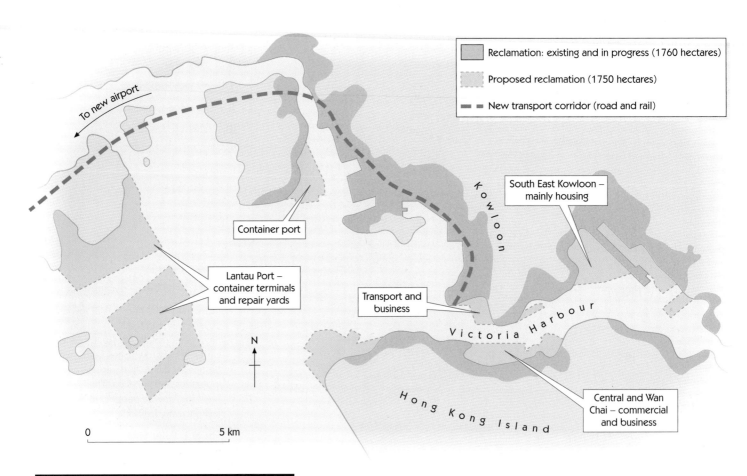

Figure 11.13: Reclamation projects in inner Hong Kong

The case for

1 Forecasts of space demand are greater than land supply (Figure 11.14).
2 Living space needs: population is expected to grow by 1.5 million by 2011. The people will need homes and open space.
3 Economic space needs: Hong Kong is the largest port for the rapidly growing countries of South East Asia. So, the container port has to be much larger. International companies need new office and business buildings. There is a shortage of hotels, conference and entertainment facilities.
4 Prestige location: Victoria Harbour is a world-famous setting for a business district. Land is very expensive, but developers are keen to invest because they can get very high rents and profits.
5 Competition: cities such as Singapore and Shanghai are trying hard to take business and trade from Hong Kong. Therefore Hong Kong must expand and build new facilities.
6 Reduce traffic congestion: goods, materials, vehicles and people need to be able to move around (Figure 11.15). New roads and public transport infrastructure must be built.
7 More jobs and more money: at least 300,000 jobs will be created. These will bring at least £25 billion extra money to Hong Kong.

▼ **Question**

5 From the information and Figure 11.14, write a brief report supporting the reclamation programme.➔

	Housing and open space	Administration and business	Industry	Port facilities	Transport	Total
Land to be made available in existing plans (supply)	558	208	110	1020	404	2300
Forecasts of land needs (demand)	700	250	400	1100	450	2650

NB
i) These figures do not include the new Chek Lap Kok Airport. ii) The forecasts are for a 'medium' rate of growth.

Figure 11.14: Reclaimed land balance sheet (hectares)

Figure 11.15: Congestion is severe throughout inner Hong Kong

Save our harbour

▼ Three questions: Who *needs* it? Is it *desirable*? Are there *alternatives*?

▼ Over 500 hectares of our wonderful harbour have gone. Now they want another 730 hectares.

▼ Victoria Harbour is world famous; it is part of Hong Kong's heritage.

▼ Water pollution will get worse if the channel is made narrower by the infill. Less water + more buildings + more people = more water pollution.

▼ At least 400 million cubic metres of offshore sand will be dredged and dumped in the harbour. This will affect the ecosystem of the harbour and the coastal waters, including valuable fisheries.

▼ This is one of the busiest harbours in the world. If it gets narrower, it will be more dangerous.

▼ They say one-quarter of the new land will be for homes and open space. But this is expensive land – only the rich will live here.

▼ It will bring even more jobs into the central areas. This means more travelling, more congestion.

▼ Why not build in the New Territories? This is where so many people live already.

Figure 11.16: Threats to Victoria Harbour, from the 'Save our Harbour' group

The case against

▼ Questions

6 Environmental groups often give out what they call 'briefing documents' to journalists. These documents sum up their case or position on a particular issue. Figure 11.16 is an example of a briefing document. Read it carefully, then write an article (not more than 200 words) for a newspaper. (Think of the type of newspaper you are writing for; use the language a journalist would use; compose an 'eye-catching' headline; use a software package and computer to design the article, if possible.)

7 Making a decision: Write briefly about what you would do to solve the problem of Victoria Harbour, giving your reasons. ➡

Figure 11.17: Busy Victoria Harbour – freighters, ferries, fishing boats and pleasure craft all crowd through this narrow harbour

Review

● The Hong Kong population of nearly 7 million is forecast to increase by 1.5 million within 15 years.
● Planning policy for growth has included both dispersal and concentration of people and jobs.
● The physical site and setting of Hong Kong makes further growth difficult.
● Land reclamation is an important part of planning policy but has created much controversy, especially over Victoria Harbour, which is surrounded by the CBD.

12

Ownership or stewardship?

Key ideas

● Increasing demand for world resources means there is more competition for those resources.

● People need to find better ways of sharing and conserving world resources.

● The management of Antarctica is an example of international stewardship but is it sustainable?

Main activity

Getting to grips with values. Extended writing about tourist development and international stewardship in the context of Antarctica.

The number of people in the world continues to grow. Each person hopes that the quality of her or his life will improve. Many of these improvements mean increasing demands upon world resources. For example, the USA has 4% of the world's population but consumes 22% of the world's energy output (Figure 12.1). In contrast, China has 25% of the world's population and consumes only 9% of the world's energy (Figure 12.2). Only a small proportion of Chinese people at present own cars or have homes with central heating or air conditioning. As their standards of living rise towards those of the United States, they will make huge demands upon the world's resources.

Figure 12.1: A crowded US freeway – most American families own at least one car and their lifestyles depend on using them

Figure 12.2: Moving around in a Chinese city, 1996: in 20 years' time, many of these people may own cars and better equipped homes

Because world resources are limited while demand is growing, competition for these resources will become more intense. A number of the case studies in this book have shown what is happening. For example:

● Land and living space for humans: Hong Kong and New York (Unit 11); Copiapo Valley, Chile (Unit 8).
● Land and living space for other species: Bosque del Apache and Yellowstone (Unit 3); the CAMPFIRE project, Zimbabwe (Unit 4).
● Energy: Oil in Oman and Alaska (Unit 5).
● Food: The fish of Prince William Sound, Alaska (Unit 4); Bangladesh and Vietnam (Unit 8).

Do we need to change the way we think?

In 1997 a world conference was held in Kyoto, Japan. A primary aim of the conference was to set targets for reducing the release of carbon dioxide and other gases into the atmosphere. Most scientists believe that these emissions are causing **global warming**. Most governments of the 170 countries attending also agree with this conclusion. They agree, too, that all parts of the world are interrelated or interdependent and that an answer must come through international co-operation. Yet agreement on what to do has proved almost impossible because each country puts its own interests first (Figure 12.3).

The country which 'owns' resources, e.g. land, forests, minerals, believes it has the right to exploit them. This means using them or selling them to other countries or foreign businesses. For example, the Indonesian government allows Japanese timber companies to buy and fell large areas of Indonesia's tropical rainforest, despite the protests of international environmental groups. We may think internationally, but all too often we act nationally. Because of this, one country's actions can lead to problems in another country. In 1997 the result of massive forest fires in Indonesia was an unhealthy smoke haze (smog) in neighbouring Malaysia.

There are only two parts of planet earth which are not legally owned by individual countries. These are the oceans beyond coastal territorial waters and the continent of Antarctica. This case study looks at what is happening in Antarctica. It allows you to consider whether we can change our thinking about resources and environments – a change from ownership ('It's mine now') to stewardship ('It's ours, now and for the future').

A European
We must cut our CO$_2$ emissions by 20% within the next 15 years to slow down global warming, or sea levels will rise and flood coastal cities.

An Indian
Most of our people don't have the luxuries of life. Why shouldn't we have the lifestyles you Americans and Europeans enjoy? To do this we have to increase our use of energy. It's up to you to cut down your carbon dioxide emissions.

An Australian
Coal is one of the main exports. Thousands of jobs and huge sums of money would be lost if they close down coal-fired power stations. I'm not convinced about all these global warming forecasts anyway.

An American
I don't think the American people will want to change their lifestyles. They love their cars, their air conditioning, central heating and all their electronic gadgets.

Figure 12.3: Views on controlling global warming

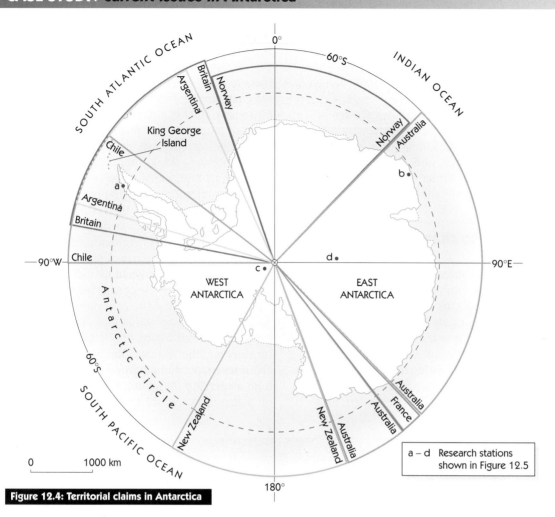

Figure 12.4: Territorial claims in Antarctica

a – d Research stations shown in Figure 12.5

FACTFILE: Antarctica

Area	12 million square kilometres (twice the size of Australia)
Average height above sea level	2300 metres (on average the highest continent)
Surface	98% ice; 2% rock with some vegetation
Ice sheet	30 million cubic kilometres; average thickness 2.3 kilometres with a maximum of 5 kilometres
Age	Up to 3 million years
Landmass	East Antarctica – a continuous landmass, about two-thirds of the total area; West Antarctica – with the ice removed this would be a string of islands (an archipelago)
Climate	A cold desert – annual snowfall on the central plateaus is the water equivalent of 50 millimetres; this increases to 500 millimetres around the fringes of the continent
Population	There is still no permanent human population; around 1000 scientists stay over the long winter and there are 4000 during the short summer
Location	1000 kilometres to South America; 4000 kilometres to Australia
Limits	The oceans, land and ice south of 60°S latitude

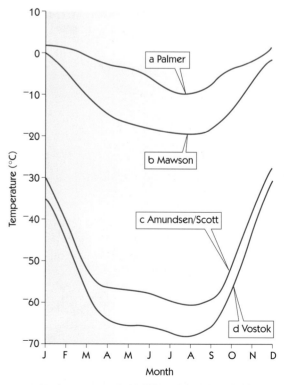

Figure 12.5: Temperature at four research stations in Antarctica

How is Antarctica administered?

Antarctica is the only continent without a permanent human population. When European explorers such as Captain Cook discovered the continent over 200 years ago, there were no existing people. Only in Antarctica, therefore, did Europeans not have to conquer or control native populations. Today there are no **aboriginal** land and culture rights to consider. So:

No native peoples
No settlers from
other continents

} = No national ownership

However, seven countries from the developed world do have longstanding 'claims' on Antarctica, which slice up the continent like a cake (Figure 12.4). None of the 'claims' are accepted as legal by other countries, so no one 'owns' Antarctica.

The continent is managed and administered by an international agency. This is based on the 1959 Antarctic Treaty. It was signed originally by 12 countries with interests in the continent. By 1995 there were over 40 countries. This Antarctic Treaty System works by international co-operation, using 14 'Articles' or principles set out in the treaty. Here are four of the most important principles:

● Antarctica is to be used for peaceful purposes only.
● The treaty does not support or deny any territorial claims by individual nations.
● International co-operation in scientific research will be encouraged.
● The Treaty System is open to any member of the United Nations.

This treaty was given greater strength in 1991 by countries agreeing to what is called the Madrid Protocol. (The full name of this agreement is the Antarctic Treaty on Environmental Protection, which was signed in Madrid.) It focuses on protecting and conserving the environment on the continent and in the surrounding oceans.

A further outcome of the treaty is that the member countries of the Antarctic Treaty System act as stewards rather than owners of Antarctica. Stewardship means caring for environmental resources on behalf of all people, now and into the future.

How are Antarctica's resources used, and not used?

The countries with 'claims' on Antarctica have always realised that the climate is far too severe for people to be able to settle there (Figure 12.5). So why have they fought hard to retain their 'claims'? The answer lies in the potential for economic profit. For example, although exploration is far from complete, there are known to be a range of useful minerals (Figure 12.6). None the less, the treaty countries agreed in 1988 to ban all mining for 50 years. This sounds like a good example of international co-operation to protect the environment. However, the large mining corporations accept that the huge costs of mining in these harsh conditions makes it uneconomic – at present anyway! The real test of the strength of international agreements will come if very valuable and rare minerals are found.

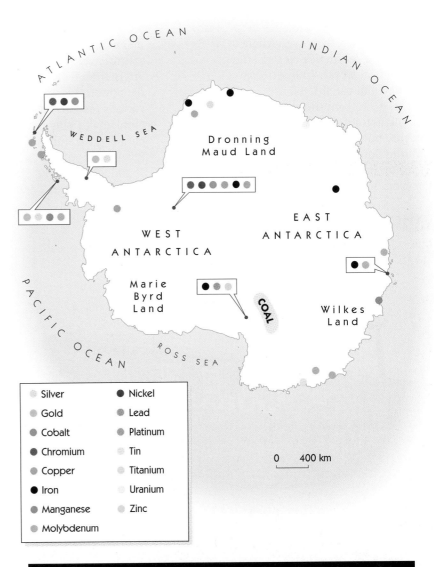

Silver	Nickel
Gold	Lead
Cobalt	Platinum
Chromium	Tin
Copper	Titanium
Iron	Uranium
Manganese	Zinc
Molybdenum	

Figure 12.6: Known mineral reserves of Antarctica (the exploration is incomplete, so there may be more)

There are, however, three present-day resource uses which allow us to assess the strengths and weaknesses of the international stewardship approach:
- scientific research and conservation;
- commercial fishing;
- tourism.

Scientific research and conservation

Many people claim that the best use for Antarctica is as a **global laboratory**. Their thinking goes like this:
- We need to be able to measure the effects that human activities are having on the global environment.
- To do this we need to find a place which is unaffected by human activity. We can then compare this environment with others.
- Antarctica, because of its size, lack of settlement and remoteness, is the natural, unpolluted place we need.
- Also, we know that the climate of Antarctica influences weather and climate patterns throughout the world. Changes in the Antarctic will affect human lives everywhere.
- Finally, in Antarctica we can study ecosystems at work within extreme environmental conditions.

In 1996, 16 countries had a total of 48 research stations in Antarctica (Figure 12.7), from tiny huts to the massive US base at McMurdo Sound. The scientists have been successful in developing international co-operation. It all began in 1957 with the International Geophysical Year programme of research. The idea of collaboration was built into the 1959 treaty and again into the 1991 Madrid Protocol. Even during the Cold War years in the 1960s and 1970s, when the USA and the USSR were in opposition, their scientists shared information and worked together.

There is evidence, however, that even scientific research causes pollution. For example:
- In 1989, an Argentine supply ship spilt 773,000 litres of fuel at Palmer Station, killing much sea life and ruining several research projects.
- Gales blew a Peruvian research ship onto rocks near King George Island, causing an oil slick a kilometre long.
- In 1993, the US government spent $1 million on a clean-up operation around McMurdo, and, recently, Greenpeace has been clearing rubbish from some sites.

Pollution and environmental damage are difficult to control because the international agreements are not legally enforceable. Only the individual national governments have legal control over their countries' stations. There is no international agency with either the money or the power to watch over the activities of the various research stations. There is also the problem of rising costs. Several countries are reducing the number of their stations, including Russia and Australia (Figure 12.8). The abandoned stations may then lie derelict or be used for tourism.

Figure 12.7: An Argentinian research base on King George Island

AUSTRALIAN TOURISTS IN ANTARCTICA?

By Robert Milliken

In the biggest reassessment of its operations in Antarctica since the end of the Cold War, Australia has proposed closing two of its three research bases on the continent and turning them into summer bases for adventure tourists.

Britain, New Zealand and Russia already allow tourists to visit Antarctica, but only by ship. There are occasional tourist flights over the continent from Australia and New Zealand, but up to now no tourists have been allowed to camp there because of fears for the security of penguin rookeries and other features of Antarctica's delicate ecosystem.

Now, Australia's Antarctic Science Advisory Committee, a government body, has recommended that Australia should consolidate the scientific research done at its Casey and Mawson bases at the third base, Davis, and set up a regular air link between Australia and the Davis base, leasing the other two to other countries or allowing tourists to go there on strictly controlled expeditions.

Australia is one of seven countries with territorial claims to Antarctica, with Argentina, Britain, Chile, France, New Zealand and Norway.

The Australian claim covers about 43 per cent of the continent, almost as much as Australia itself. Its operations in Antarctica reflect the Cold War era, when countries that signed the Antarctic Treaty in 1959 were keen to protect their patches from encroachment by others.

But this has been an expensive business. Australia's three bases are about 1,000km apart from each other, each with its own transport system and infrastructure. These logistics consume two-thirds of Canberra's Antarctic budget of about A$60m (£26m) a year, leaving only one-third for the bases' real purpose: research on world climate change, sea life, glaciers, space physics and human impact on Antarctica.

Figure 12.8: Australia thinks again

Commercial fishing

The marine ecosystem of the Antarctic oceans is extremely rich and diverse. These resources have been exploited for almost 200 years. Until recently, this has been a story of uncontrolled and unsustainable use. During the nineteenth century, sealing and whaling stations were set up on the edge of the continent. By the 1870s, some species, such as the fur seal, had been hunted almost to extinction. Whale catches increased to unsustainable levels once factory ships were introduced in the 1920s. These larger vessels could process the heavy mammals at sea, without having to tow them to the shore stations. As a result the numbers of one whale species after another 'crashed' as new types were hunted after stocks of one type were reduced. Only in 1986 did the International Whaling Commission manage to ban all whaling, to allow whale numbers to recover. Yet through the 1990s the main whaling nations, Japan and Norway, campaigned to begin whaling once more.

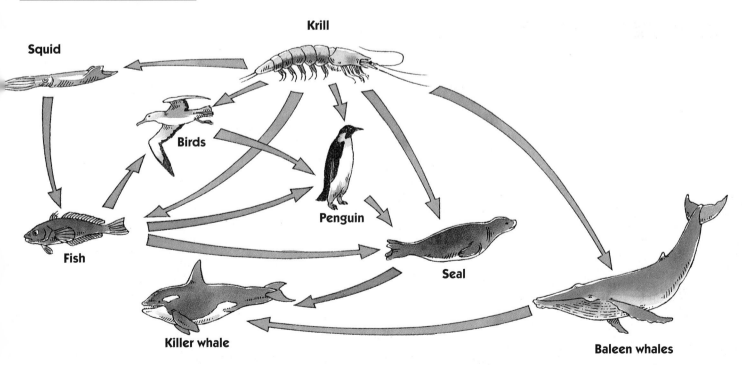

Figure 12.9: Krill – the foundation of Antarctica's marine food web

As one type of resource has been used up, the fishing industry has turned to other species. As the whale stocks became exhausted, fish such as mackerel and cod were overfished; when the fish catch fell, the fleets turned to krill. This stripping of krill from the seas is particularly dangerous as krill – a type of shrimp – form the foundation of the marine food web (Figure 12.9).

Once more, only after the crisis has arrived, has international action taken place. Fisheries are now regulated by the 1982 Convention for the Conservation of Antarctic Marine Resources (CCAMR). This limits fish catches to 100,000 tonnes a year, and krill catches to 1.5 million tonnes.

In this case, therefore, the verdict on how international stewardship has worked is: 'Too little, almost too late.' Remember, however, that the size and remoteness of the oceans make control of the ships from so many countries very difficult. Conservationists hope that a World Marine Park can be created in Antarctica to act as a refuge for threatened species such as the great whales.

Tourism

Liz and Brian Lister: 'We went to Antarctica for two reasons: it's the final wilderness and the wildlife is fantastic. It was the experience of a lifetime.'

The latest wave of people attracted by the environmental resources of Antarctica are adventure tourists. The first tourists came in 1957, but only since the mid-1980s have numbers begun increasing rapidly (Figure 12.10). Almost all of the tourists arrive by cruise ship and are taken onto the continent by Zodiac inflatable boats or by helicopter for short visits. The attractions are the animal and bird colonies (Figure 12.11); the wild, magnificent scenery; historic sites such as the old whaling stations and explorers' huts; and the scientific research stations.

Figure 12.11: Are these tourists following the Antarctic Traveller's Code (see Figure 12.13)?

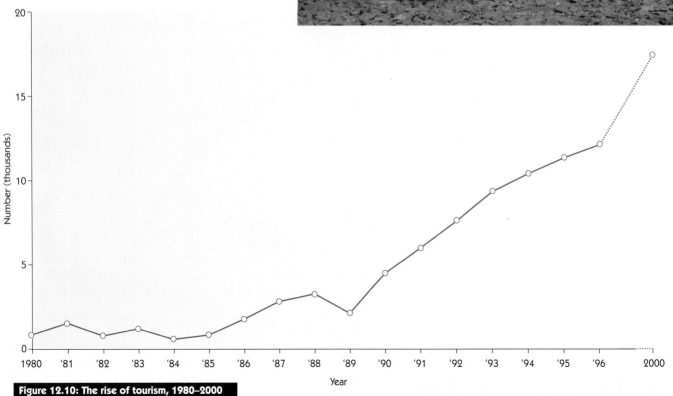

Figure 12.10: The rise of tourism, 1980–2000

As numbers increase, the environmental impacts increase (Figure 12.12). Five aspects are causing particular concern:

● The size of cruise ships is increasing. Until 1993 the largest vessel carried less than 500 tourists. In 1995, cruise ships with more than 1000 people were arriving. This increases the concentration of people in a small area.

● The tourist season is November to January, during the short Antarctic summer. This is also when the birds and animals are breeding, and are particularly sensitive to disturbance.

● The tourists land on a small number of ice free sites, i.e. where the wildlife, the vegetation and the scientists are concentrated.

● The vegetation of lichens and mosses is fragile and very slow to recover from impacts.

● There is still no permanent tourist accommodation on the continent itself, but the tourism industry and some national governments are keen to change this (Figure 12.8).

As with the other resource uses, the key problem for tourism is who should and can control how the industry uses Antarctica's resources. The ships and the tour operators come from different countries. In 1991 they formed the International Association of Antarctic Tour Operators (IAATO) and have agreed to adopt a code of conduct (Figure 12.13). However, these are guidelines – not laws, not all operators and ship owners have joined, and it is not clear who is to monitor whether the tour guides keep to the guidelines.

Type of activity	Nature of impacts	Infrastructure characteristics
Overflights	● Fallout from engines; disturbance of wildlife due to noise	● No requirement for permanent land-based facilities
Ship-based	● Transient environmental effects, although pressure may be placed on regularly visited land attractions; oil spills; disturbance to wildlife; potential introduction of bird and plant diseases and exotic flora	● No requirement for permanent land-based facilities; some permanent moorings may be established at frequently visited locations
Onshore facilities	● Increased demands for ice-free land and fresh water supply; disposal of sewage and rubbish; degradation of specific sites with high visitation levels; disturbance to wildlife; potential introduction of bird and plant diseases and exotic flora ● Possible damage to cultural heritage sites ● Aesthetic impacts	● Support infrastructure including the provision of an all-weather air strip capable of handling large commercial aircraft; accommodation facilities; potential combination of tourist facilities with scientific bases; development of interpretative facilities and associated infrastructure such as boardwalks and signs

Figure 12.12: Environmental impacts of tourism in Antarctica

Antarctic visitors

- MUST *NOT* leave footprints in fragile mosses, lichens or grasses.
- MUST *NOT* dump plastic or other, non biodegradable garbage overboard or onto the continent.
- MUST *NOT* violate the seals', penguins' or seabirds' Personal Space
  - ○ start with a 'baseline' distance of 15ft (5m) from penguins, seabirds, and true seals and 60ft (18m) from fur seals
  - ○ give animals right of way
  - ○ stay on the edge of, and don't walk through, animal groups
  - ○ back off if necessary
  - ○ never touch the animals.
- MUST *NOT* interfere with protected areas or scientific research.
- MUST *NOT* take souvenirs.

Antarctic tour companies

- SHOULD apply the Antarctic Traveller's Code to all officers, crew, staff and passengers.
- SHOULD utilise one (1) guide or leader for every twenty (20) passengers.
- SHOULD employ experienced and sensitive on-board leadership.
- SHOULD use vessels that are safe for Antarctic ice conditions.
- SHOULD adopt a shipwide anti-dumping pledge.

Figure 12.13: Antarctic Traveller's Code

▼ Questions

1 What did the Antarctic Treaty set out to achieve?
2 a What is meant by a global laboratory?
  b Why is a global laboratory not necessarily the way forward for Antarctica?
3 a What is krill?
  b Why will Baleen whales die out if krill is overfished?
  c What could happen to Antarctica's ecosystem if krill is overfished?
4 *Either*: A European travel company has plans to offer cruise holidays with Antarctica 'stop-overs'. Write advice for the company on how they should be thinking about their plans.
  Or: Design an informative single sheet to send to a travel company which is planning to start cruise holidays to Antarctica. The sheet should contain detailed information on the fragility of Antarctica's environment.
5 From the point of view of an environment campaign group such as Friends of the Earth or Greenpeace, write about the need to save Antarctica. Explain the ideas of international stewardship and suggest that people need to explore genuine co-operative working practices which are not based on the commercialisation of the continent. ◆

Review

Antarctica is a huge continent which is not under the legal ownership of any individual country. Therefore, it is perhaps the world's best chance of testing whether the idea of stewardship of global resources can work. At present, the continent is managed and administered by international agencies. Most operate through agreements rather than laws. This makes effective control in these remote and extreme environments very difficult.

Glossary

A

Aboriginal — Refers to the native people of a region. *89*

Aftershocks — Minor tremors which occur following the main earthquake shocks. *13*

Air mass — A large body of air with similar temperature and humidity levels. *19*

D

Desalination — The removal of salt from seawater. *41*

Development — The process of economic growth and improvements in quality of life in a region or country. *46*

E

Epicentre — The point on the earth's surface directly above the site of an earthquake. *13*

Ecosystem — A system that shows the relationships between a community of living things (plants and animals) and their non-living environments. *23*

F

Fault zone — A narrow belt of the earth's crust caused by the breaking or shearing of rocks as a result of the application of enormous forces. *13*

Flyway — A path followed regularly by flocks of migrating birds. *24*

G

Geyser — A column of steam and superheated water thrown up through a hole in the ground. *28*

Global laboratory — Used to describe the role of Antarctica as a laboratory to study environmental changes taking place on planet earth. *90*

Global warming — The predicted slow increase in atmospheric temperatures throughout the world. *64*

Globalisation — The process by which businesses and industries are organised on a world scale. *50*

H

Habitat — The home environment of a living creature or species. *23*

Hollowing out — The process whereby companies move their production abroad, while retaining their headquarters and decision making in the 'home' country. *53*

Hurricane — An extreme form of low pressure system with wind speeds in excess of 120kph which occurs mainly in tropical and sub-tropical latitudes; known in the Pacific as cyclones or typhoons. *21*

Hypocentre — The location of an earthquake, usually below the surface in the earth's crust. *13*

I

Impoundment — An enclosure surrounded by embankments to hold in water as part of a water management scheme. *26*

International migrant — A person who moves from one country to another to live. *65*

Inter-Tropical Convergence Zone (ITCZ) — The zone of low pressure between the Tropics where the North East and South East Trade winds meet; also known as the Equatorial Trough. *19*

K

Keiretsu — A large Japanese industrial corporation. *52*

L

Lahar	A mud flow from a volcanic eruption. *10*
Land reclamation	The improvement of land, usually by draining, infilling, levelling or decontamination. *82*
Levee	A natural or constructed bank alongside a river. *58*

M

Meteorological	To do with weather conditions. *16*
Metropolitan core	The central area of a large city or metropolis, with a dense concentration of businesses. *77*
Monoculture	The growing of a single crop throughout an area over a period of years. *64*
Multinational corporation	A large company which operates in a number of countries; also known as a 'transnational corporation'. *50*

N

Net migration balance	The balance between immigration and emigration. *66*
Non-renewable resource	A resource which does not replace itself after use. *32*
Non-sustainable	When more of a resource is being exploited than is being replaced. *32*

P

Periphery	The outer districts of a large city or metropolis. *77*
Permafrost	Permanently frozen ground found in cold environments. *44*
Plate margins	Junction zones between tectonic plates of the earth's crust. *9*
Predator	A species, e.g. animal, bird, fish, which hunts other species. *28*
Productive capacity	The weight or volume or growth of living matter produced by an ecosystem in a certain period, e.g. a year. *31*
Pyroclastic	Materials thrown out in a solid form by volcanic eruptions. *10*

R

Renewable resource	A resource which can replace itself after use. *30*

S

Scale	The ratio of the distance on a map to the actual distance on the ground. *73*
Seismologist	A scientist who studies the movement and patterns of shockwaves from earthquakes and explosions as they move through the earth's interior. *13*
Species	Living organisms which can breed with each other. *23*
Subsistence economy	A way of life where people live off what they produce for themselves. *32*
Sustainable	A form of use where resources are conserved over time. *30*
Symbols key	An explanation of the symbols used on a map. *73*

T

Trade barrier	When a country or group of countries put tariffs on imported materials and goods in order to protect their own industries. *54*
Transnational corporation	See Multinational corporation.
'Transplant'	A factory built by a transnational company in a country other than where it has its headquarters. *53*
Trophic level	A level of feeding and energy in a food chain. *23*
Tundra	An ecosystem of shrubs and low vegetation found in cold environments. *44*

W

Wetland	Marshy areas which are a habitat for wildlife. *23*